About the author

GW00500687

Between 1987 and 1995, Peter Luff was Director of the European Movement in the United Kingdom and then Deputy Secretary-General and Vice President of the International European Movement. Born in Brussels and educated in Britain, he took a degree in politics and international relations at the University College of Wales, Swansea, and travelled around the world for eighteen months before taking the post of Assistant Director of Amnesty International UK. While at Amnesty, he produced the first two in the series of comedy shows that became known as *The Secret Policeman's Ball* and helped to found the all-party Parliamentary Human Rights Group. After brief spells with the BBC's *World About Us* series and Survival International, he became Funding and Marketing Director of the Social Democratic Party.

Peter Luff has broadcast regularly on radio and television and in 1992 wrote the *Simple Guide to the Maastricht Treaty* whose success encouraged him to try and unravel the themes and issues underlying the present Intergovernmental Conference. A Fellow of the Royal Society of Arts and Manufactures and the Royal Geographical Society, he is married with four children and is a Director of Matrix Communications Consultancy Ltd.

> *This book is dedicated to my parents, uncles and aunts whose courage and sacrifice in two world wars and subsequent commitment to reconciliation meant that their children and grandchildren were given the greatest gift of all – the chance to grow up in peace and security.*

About the author

A Brilliant Conspiracy?

Britain and the Federal Debate in Europe

PETER LUFF

The Greycoat Press

Contents

Preface

When I began this book I intended it to be a simple guide to the Intergovernmental Conference (IGC). My aim was very straightforward: to provide anyone who wanted it with enough information to express their view about the kind of Europe they wanted. It seemed to me that what was most necessary today was an informed debate about Europe in which everyone who wanted to could take part.

My experience addressing small and large groups throughout the country convinced me that what people really wanted was clear information. Not just the official documentation provided by the European institutions but something that put it all into context. What people needed was both a historical context and a conceptual framework into which they could fit the facts they read in the press, heard on radio or saw on television.

It was quite clear at the time of the Maastricht Treaty, for instance, that one reason why that document was so impenetrable was because its purpose was to amend the previous treaties that had been adopted over the past forty years. But if one didn't know what was in the previous treaties, then the amendments were utterly meaningless and the Treaty itself was viewed, unsurprisingly, with deep suspicion. Without some idea as to the ultimate purpose of European integration and the reason for its creation, the potential loss of certain areas of sovereignty traditionally associated with the nation state was bound to provoke anger and hostility.

Having produced a first draft of a simple guide, however, I began to realise that this wasn't enough. Information alone would not be sufficient to combat the extraordinary and growing volume of misinformation that had begun to dominate the European debate. I felt a mounting anger that the truth was being twisted to the point where the argument for a united Europe might actually be lost.

Not only was the government giving ground daily to the onslaught of some of its Euro-phobic back-benchers, there was also a failure on the part of convinced Europeans to make their case effectively.

The problem seemed to be that the protagonists of a united Europe ran away from offering a clear vision. Rather than having a strategic objective for which we could fight on our own terms, we were confronting our opponents on territory of their own choosing and losing a succession of small, but in the context serious, skirmishes. The time had arrived to be clearer about our objectives and to remember exactly why the need for European Union was as great as ever.

There will always be politicians ready to use nationalism as a means of either clinging to power or obtaining it. They will not worry about its long term implications so long as it meets their immediate needs. That they might put the stability of Europe at risk, once again, is either dismissed as irrelevant or regarded as a small price to pay.

Modern Europe was built by those who had experienced first hand the tragedy of war. Resistance leaders, who had shared with colleagues across the continent the fear of being hunted, tortured and killed, knew that there had to be a better alternative than war for settling future disputes. A number of them were prominent at the post-war Congress of Europe which took the first steps towards building a united Europe. Unfortunately, just as the UK government recently did not see fit to honour the last remaining survivors of the Battle of the Somme, it may be that their experience and their sacrifice will also be forgotten.

Remembering is not merely a matter of sentiment, but of hard commonsense. Europe must never fall into the trap of thinking that continental war is no longer possible. There will always be self-seeking politicians who will place vanity and ambition above the requirements of stability and security. What we need is a system which prevents them from fulfilling their ambitions.

Of course, Europe must change and develop. It must become more open, accountable and responsive to its citizens. It must be reformed. This can be done, but it will require a renewed sense of purpose.

Author's note

The following chapters offer a simple guide to the arguments that will be raised during the course of the IGC. In order to make them more understandable, I have included a short history of the European Union and the treaties that brought it into being and a brief description of the main institutions and their functions.

I have used the terms *pro-European* and *Eurosceptic* to describe the main strands of opinion on many of the issues raised in this book. These terms cannot clearly identify every variety of political thought. The major issue is whether or not the countries of Europe should move towards closer political, economic and monetary union. Although many of those opposed to European Union welcome some form of loose free-trade association, their rhetoric has frequently reflected a nationalism that has not unreasonably been construed as anti-European. It has certainly struck many of our European partners that way.

I am extremely grateful for all the help and advice I have received from many people who share this belief in the importance of a united Europe, many of them for much longer than I. In particular I should like to thank Lord Cobbold for having substantially re-written the chapter on economic and monetary union; Dr Martyn Bond and Julie Smith; my predecessor at the European Movement, Ernest Wistrich, and my successor, Stephen Woodard, for their invaluable suggestions and criticisms; my partners at Matrix Communications, Dick Newby and Graham Johnson, both for their amendments of the text and for their patience in helping me through innumerable revisions; Edward Mortimer for the title; my publisher, Oliver Bond, for his enthusiasm and patience; Andrew Duff for his advice and suggestions; and, above all, John Pinder, whose vision, knowledge and dedication has sustained generations of European federalists.

Although the book could not have been written without their support and contributions, the views expressed are those of the author and are not necessarily shared by those listed.

1. A new conspiracy

It is hardly surprising that the opponents of European union – the Eurosceptics – have dominated the debate since the Maastricht Treaty was ratified. Their simplistic sloganeering has been a gift to headline writers. With an enviable freedom to choose their targets at will and no need to offer serious alternatives for detailed analysis, their strident attacks on the principles and institutions of European union, combined with the government's absurd posturing during its self-imposed BSE crisis and the persistent xenophobia displayed in some sections of the tabloid press, has sown widespread confusion and left much of the pro-European lobby deeply demoralised.

The question is why has such a crass campaign been so effective if, as the supporters of European integration believe, Europe is so obviously "a good thing"? One reason, of course, is that it is considerably easier to attack an idea or an institution in a 30 second sound-bite than it is to defend one. It does not require much subtlety or sophistication to accuse supra-national institutions of being remote, unresponsive and dictatorial. To explain the nature of these institutions, their political evolution and the problems they face in terms of both operation and communication, however, requires time and concentration – commodities not usually on offer in the media. During the Maastricht Treaty debate, I was telephoned by a researcher on BBC's *Newsnight* programme asking me to explain the meaning of federalism in the context of the treaty. In the ten minute conversation that followed, I thought I did quite well and was flattered to be asked to record an interview on the subject. "But can you shorten it a bit?" the researcher asked. "How long do I have?" "Twenty seconds!" was the reply.

Similarly, I was asked by a well-known journalist if I could provide him with a five minute summary of the Maastricht Treaty itself. The problem was not only that he had not bothered to obtain a copy himself but also that he had not the faintest idea what was in either the Treaty of Rome or the Single European Act (SEA), both of which Maastricht was designed to amend.

But to blame the media alone for the serious difficulties facing the defenders of European integration would be absurd. What the Maastricht Treaty revealed was the degree to which those who are convinced of the fundamental importance of building a united Europe have failed to persuade the mass of people, particularly in the UK, of the strength and vitality of their case. The reality is that the attacks of the Eurosceptics have been falling on fertile ground.

I believe that there are three fundamental reasons for this. The first is the enormous gap between the political, administrative and business classes who have daily contact with their continental counterparts and most ordinary people to whom the purpose, institutions and processes of the European Union have never been fully explained. Not only do many people feel ill-informed about even the basic facts – for example which countries are in the Union and which of the institutions make and execute decisions at the European level – they are also conscious that, as the whole process develops and deepens, the gap between those who understand it and those who do not is in danger of becoming unbridgeable.

Financial Times journalist Edward Mortimer has called the creation of the European Union, "a brilliant conspiracy of political elites". It may be that as ordinary people struggled to rebuild their lives, homes and jobs in the aftermath of two catastrophic and bloody world wars, a conspiracy was necessary. The task at hand was the reconstruction of a devastated continent.

It required the courage and vision of leaders prepared to take risks to find concrete and lasting ways to prevent war. Waiting for the results of what would have been long and bitter public debates, clouded by grief and anger, might have lost forever the unique opportunity for reconciliation that presented itself. Instead, they seized the moment and began the experiment of binding victors and vanquished into a Community of common purpose. It was certainly a brilliant conspiracy for which we, who have benefited from the longest period of peace and prosperity Europe has seen in modern history, have cause to be grateful.

But although we owe a debt of gratitude to those who had the skill and judgment to translate their vision into solid economic achievement and workable institutions, there has been a dangerous tendency on the part of many convinced Europeans to live in the past and to fail to appreciate how much the world has changed since the heady and adventurous days of the immediate post-war period. In today's world, people, living in the midst of an ever-accelerating technological revolution, are no longer prepared to follow either individual leaders or ideologies blindly. With vast amounts of information available from the traditional media and at the touch of a keyboard, the whole concept of leadership is being re-examined. Consultation is recognised as a fundamental tool of management. It is increasingly recognised in business that for a project to succeed, there needs to be a high level of understanding and commitment at every level of the organisation. Yet in politics and the management of national and international affairs, consultation, apart from periodic elections conducted in a hysterical climate of mutual mud-slinging, is proffered grudgingly in the face of irresistible pressure from disgruntled voters, if considered at all. Unfortunately, this fundamental shift in public awareness was not fully grasped by those who drafted, negotiated, signed and then tried to persuade their electorates to accept the Maastricht Treaty.

Andrew Marr quite rightly asks, in his analysis of Britain's constitutional plight, *Ruling Britannia*:

> Was it democratically right to agree a binding political settlement at Maastricht so long and involved that no ordinary, and few specialist, voters could understand it? This is a problem which concerns people at both ends of the political spectrum. The Scottish socialist writer and poet Tom Leonard made the key point when he cited the great English radical Tom Paine: 'The enemy of democracy,' Paine argued, 'was the mystification of government because it makes equality of dialogue impossible.' With mystification, one might add, comes the caste that can be called the Keepers of the Mystery. Just as abstraction is the economic enemy, so mystification is the political one.

A BRILLIANT CONSPIRACY?

There is a real danger that Europe's political elites have become the "Keepers of the Mystery". Their failure to provide people with the information on which to make up their minds and then to have their say, and to listen to the result, is taking its toll. In a recent article suggesting that previous support for European integration among European citizens had now turned to 'Europhobia', *Newsweek* magazine suggested "that even in France and Germany," the indispensable core nations for monetary union, "anger is stirring against the 'big guys'." And so it should. Until they recognise that the next step is not another treaty or grand conference but a commitment to explain fully what has already been agreed, as well as future options, the erosion of public confidence in the whole idea of Europe can only get worse.

The great irony, however, is that the traditional European elites, especially those working within the institutions, are being attacked with such ferocity just as they have begun to take these problems seriously and are searching for new and imaginative ways to disseminate information and stimulate a wider public debate. After all, proposals that aim to tackle head-on many of the complaints about the Union's underlying lack of transparency and accountability are on the agenda of the IGC. Indeed, one of the main aims of the Conference is to find a way to make the European Union more open and responsive to its citizens. The Reflection Group, set up to examine various options in advance of the Conference itself, outlined a whole raft of proposals to open the institutions up to greater scrutiny and to provide the information necessary to widen and deepen public participation in the debate.

Surely these are reforms that should be welcomed by both sides of the European debate. If it appears that Europe's decision-makers have at last recognised the error of their ways and are about to embark upon a programme of reform, why has the criticism and abuse increased rather than diminished? As Former Foreign Minister Douglas Hurd put it in the *Sunday Times*: "It is hard to encourage Brussels to more energetic efforts if the background noises from Britain suggest this is an institution we are trying not to reform but to destroy." It seems very odd that just when things look as if they are going to get better, the degree of hostility expressed by the anti-integrationists seems to become ever more vigorous.

There seems to be something decidedly disingenuous about these attacks until one looks a little closer at their motivation. Why should opposition to the European Union be growing at a time when it appears determined to initiate measures designed to increase its democratic legitimacy, unless this is precisely what most disturbs its critics?

The way the European Union is moving today is not inimical to democratic aspirations, but quite the opposite: the vested interests that will be most affected are national governments whose ability to control events through the secretive Council of Ministers, without the disruptive intrusion of the press or parliamentarians, may be curtailed and multi-national corporations who may lose the freedom to operate across borders without adequate controls.

It is surely no coincidence that the British parliamentary opposition to further integration includes a substantial number of leading Thatcherites who share the former Prime Minister's authoritarian instincts. Underlying much of this opposition seems to be less a desire to open decision-making up to wider public participation than a last ditch struggle to retain and regain the power to control the nation state that they perceive may be slipping away forever.

The frequent calls in this country for a referendum on aspects of further integration, such as economic and monetary union, pretend that a plebiscite could be a substitute for real democratic accountability in the process of European union. As we have often been reminded, plebiscites and referenda in the wrong hands can sometimes do more to confirm authoritarian regimes than to extend democracy. What appears to be a remedy to the elitism of Europe may turn out to be no more than a confirmation that power should remain concentrated in the hands of a national elite. If this is the case, the pro-referendum campaign could well turn out to be a more dangerous and far less brilliant conspiracy than the creation of the European Union ever was.

Elitism is not confined to the European level of government: it exists at every level of politics. In its present form, the political debate is not so much concerned with the power, authority and sovereignty of the people as a struggle between political elites at different levels. One of the purposes of this book is to examine whether there may be a better alternative to this ultimately sterile struggle; whether it is possible to devise a system, applicable throughout the European Union, which would allow real power and sovereignty to be exercised by the people of Europe at the appropriate level.

The second reason for the growing reaction against European unification seems to be a new tolerance towards expressions of nationalism that would have been considered unacceptable in the immediate post-war period. Is this a popular expression of what Sir James Goldsmith calls in his book, *The Trap*, the "dominant political passion of the age ... the search for national identity"? Or, more cynically, just part of a post-modernist reaction to anything resembling political correctness? Either way, it contains some serious dangers. It may seem platitudinous to remind ourselves, yet again, of the atavistic tribal feelings that seem to lie just below the surface of every European nation, no matter how ordered or civilised it may appear on the surface, yet to fail to do so could be fatal. It is extraordinary how quickly historical resentments, fears and angers can erupt when cracks in the political and economic edifice appear.

It is wishful thinking to believe that modern Europe can somehow shake off its history simply because the majority of its people now take foreign holidays and share similar tastes in music and fashion from one end of the continent to the other. As George Orwell pointed out, channelling nationalism into sport does not necessarily diminish its underlying dangers. Reading sections of the tabloid press during Euro '96, it was hard, at times, to remember that we were not at war with Germany again.

Old resentments often die slowly and can be revived with extraordinary ease. Within living memory, the people of Europe were at war with each other. In Neal Ascherson's words, writing in the *Independent on Sunday*:

> Bosnia stirs many feelings. One of them is horror, another compassion, a third anger. But, for many Europeans, there is another underlying emotion which is more powerful than all the rest. This is fear – fear based on memory. There have been times when all Europe was a Bosnia.

This is not to suggest that all feelings of national pride and patriotism are negative or should be suppressed or hidden. Indeed quite the reverse is true. With nations as much as with individuals, the ability to make a clear and realistic assessment of needs and objectives, combined with calm assertiveness and a willingness to understand the views and needs of others, derives from a feeling of confidence and self-worth. What Britain's failure to play a prominent role in the development of the European Union and the petty posturing that has characterised so many of the government's outbursts against its partners reveal is less a secure belief in Britain's innumerable strengths and abilities than a lack of self-confidence. Fifty years ago there may have been some misguided logic behind the British belief that our unique position at the point of intersection of three circles of influence – the Commonwealth, the Atlantic Alliance and the wider Europe – freed us from the necessity of joining the European Community at its inception. But our subsequent experiences should have dispelled any such illusions by now. The greatest tragedy was our failure to join the core leadership of Europe when the Communities were initially created. To do so in the late 1990s will require a much greater effort of will and diplomacy.

The appeal of nationalism is at its greatest at times of national uncertainty and loss of self-confidence. Nationalism is not only, in Dr. Johnson's maliciously apt aphorism, "the last refuge of the scoundrel", but, in the context of the contemporary need to build a new world order based upon co-operation rather than confrontation, it can appear both dangerous and, at times, pathetic. Few people, let alone the members of the regiment itself, could have failed to be embarrassed by Michael Portillo's claim, at the 1995 Conservative Party conference, that international respect for Britain rested on the ferocity of the SAS. Not only did his speech fail to understand the intelligence and integrity of our armed forces but it carried the false bravado of an Inspector Clouseau or a Tony Hancock informing an opponent that "his hands are registered with the police".

The "Up yours, Delors!" mentality of *The Sun*, which ran a front page picture of a yob in Union Jack underpants holding two fingers up to the continent, speaks volumes about the sense of failure permeating British life. It is a source of constant amazement to many continental observers that the Britain which stood alone and confident against the might of Nazi Germany should have so swiftly become so uncertain and insecure.

The same lack of confidence shows itself in a less exaggerated form in the frequently expressed fears that deeper European integration will result in a loss of national identity. Clearly some aspects of national life will change; some have already changed. Decimalisation of coinage and the metrification of weights and measures as well as new regulations adopted in a wide variety of activities as part of single market harmonisation have affected all of us in minor or major ways at work, as consumers and in our leisure. Coming to terms with litres, metres and kilos can be frustrating and even irritating. Certainly, at times, there has been understandable resentment at the degree of bureaucracy involved in the enforcement of petty regulations, but it is well worth bearing in mind that some of these have been added to European legislation by zealots in Whitehall rather than Brussels: what is called 'gold-plating' by the national administrations.

But has it really affected our identity? Do we seriously believe that we have become less English, Scottish, Welsh or Irish because we add up in a different way or because our lawnmowers are designed to meet European specifications? Can it be that our sense of national identity is really so frail that it is threatened by the adoption of a single currency?

'Europe' has simply become a convenient scapegoat for many of the feelings of insecurity brought on by living in a rapidly changing world. In reality, a far greater threat comes from America, the cultural hegemon with whom we share a common language and whose films, music, diet and fashion have a vast influence on all areas of British life. As part and parcel of the globalisation of business, commerce and information technology this would continue even if the whole edifice of European integration were swept aside tomorrow. It is not the Commission or the European Parliament (EP) that make children eat pizza and McDonald's burgers, listen to techno-music or watch *Baywatch* and *Superman*. Nor are there European regulations forcing British pubs to produce menus offering everything from Mexican enchiladas to Indonesian satay. Indeed, one of the more foolish aspects of excessive European zeal, especially in France, has been the attempt to create artificial barriers against cultural invasion. It is a Canute-like reaction to the reality of life in an increasingly economically, socially and culturally inter-dependent world.

The trick is to find the right balance between the cultural enrichment that can result from such a wide source of stimulation and the ability to retain the values and customs that define national identity. Europe's strength is its diversity. It is a fallacy to assume that union threatens it. As Sir Winston Churchill put it in his speech at the 1948 Congress of Europe which laid the foundations of European integration:

> It is said with truth that this (the movement for European unity) involves some sacrifice or merger of national sovereignty. I prefer to regard it as the gradual assumption by all the nations concerned of that larger sovereignty which alone can protect their diverse and distinctive customs and characteristics and their national traditions, all of which under totalitarian systems, whether Nazi, Fascist, or Communist, would certainly be blotted out forever.

Today the threat may come from the inability of European nations individually to afford the cost of maintaining and developing their cultural heritage, rather than from totalitarian regimes. As Sir David Putnam has frequently stressed, the solution is not to ban or restrict American cultural imports but for Europe collectively to invest in its extraordinary and unparalleled cultural talent. The arts generally, and especially the film and television industries, do not merely provide entertainment, or even information: they provide the means whereby a culture can reflect its own behaviour and values; they create the myths that will permeate and influence the thoughts and actions of future generations.

Many pro-European intellectuals refer to European culture only in terms of the past. While it is quite clear and of profound importance that we share, as Europeans, the legacy of Michelangelo, Shakespeare, Voltaire and Beethoven, it is just as important to devote energy and resources to ensuring that contemporary European talent is able to express itself both for our own benefit and that of future generations.

I doubt very much if, for most western Europeans, the search for national identity reflects the spirit of the age. It is quite natural for citizens newly liberated from Communist totalitarian regimes that were ultimately controlled by a foreign power to express their freedom through a revival of nationalist sentiment, but the same hardly applies to men and women in West European nations for whom national identity is a comfortable and routine fact of life.

A more pressing issue, however, is whether the territory of all existing member states necessarily corresponds to national identity. If anything, this is where the European idea most threatens the British political establishment. There is a need, now enshrined in the manifesto commitments of the main opposition parties, to recognise the growing political aspirations of the constituent nations that are incorporated within the UK. It is not a coincidence that many of the most vociferous opponents of the devolution of power within the UK are also opposed to greater European integration and vice versa. Nor is it a coincidence that the Scots particularly have tended to understand the process of European Union far more pragmatically than their English neighbours. But nor is it a conspiracy to undermine the nation state. Both are part of a greater attempt to locate power and authority at the appropriate levels in order to meet the needs and desires of ordinary people. The crucial task is to find a system that allows ordinary people to express their own sovereignty at every level of government.

But the last and, I believe, the most decisive reason for the failure of pro-Europeans to carry the debate has been their failure to explain clearly and boldly exactly what the objective of European union should be and why it is of such fundamental importance to all the citizens of Europe.

There has been a tendency to treat each new issue, be it the deregulation of trade or monetary union, as a freestanding item without relating it to the bigger picture. Without a broad understanding of the Union's aims and its procedures many decisions can seem at best arbitrary and at worst hostile.

A prime example is the recent BSE crisis. The British government made it quite clear, almost to the point of obsession, that it will resist any attempt in the IGC to increase the scope of qualified majority voting in the Council of Ministers and that it will press for a reduction in the powers of the European Court and the Commission. In the case of the BSE crisis, however, it relied on the support of the Commission to find a solution and will almost certainly seek the Court's jurisdiction to ensure full compliance when an agreed way out has been reached. Furthermore, its chances of obtaining a favourable decision in the Council of Ministers would be substantially greater under qualified majority voting, rather than have the threat of any one member state exercising a veto. With such confused messages being relayed by the government, it is not surprising that there is considerable misunderstanding among the public at large.

This sense of confusion is further exacerbated by the fact that European integration is not a fixed item but is in continual evolution. Media information about Europe tends to focus on an immediate event or decision, rarely explaining the background or the context. Although there are substantially more articles on European integration in the British media than almost anywhere on the continent, there is little discussion outside the pages of some of the weightier broadsheets of the principles, aims, causes and effects of the movement towards further union. The result is like a mass of jigsaw pieces with no guiding picture to help solve the puzzle. Without a conceptual framework upon which to hang them, dribs and drabs of information, however detailed they may be, often make very little sense and are quickly forgotten.

The failure to convey the fundamental reasons behind the European idea and its ultimate objectives has allowed disillusion to reign where there should have been a sense of awe at its breathtaking achievements. By running away from the vision that set the whole process in motion and by concentrating on the details at the expense of the broader picture, pro-Europeans have played into the hands of those who know the price of everything but the value of nothing.

It is almost incredible that the central and overwhelming achievement of fifty years of peaceful co-operation in Western Europe should be overshadowed by the shape of bananas, the consistency of sausages or the subtleties of qualified majority voting. Of course such topics should be freely and openly discussed – it would be good to think that the real facts did regularly see the light of day – but they should put into proportion. Like so many subjects, the European debate has been debased by a mixture of trivialisation and exaggeration. While much of the daily constructive co-operation is routinely ignored, one badly drafted directive that implies, for example, inappropriate travelling conditions for shellfish, can grab the headlines.

As we see, perhaps for the last time, old soldiers returning to the site of the Battle of the Somme that took place 80 years ago, it is worth reminding ourselves that there are deeper issues at stake than the future of the prawn-flavoured crisp. Unless a sense of proportion can be restored, there is a profound danger that future generations will never know the underlying reasons for the whole European project.

It is necessary for those who care about Europe to lift their sights and begin to reaffirm the basic principles upon which the Community and then the Union were founded. The idealism of the founders of Europe has been ignored, while politicians have focused on the practical details of Europe's construction. The attempt to sell Europe as though it were merely about demonstrable material advantage has not been a success precisely because not all the advantages are immediately demonstrable. The strength and the weakness of the European level of government is that, by necessity, it involves compromise. The disadvantage of pooling certain powers is offset by the enormous advantages gained by sharing others. Although it is not a political zero sum game, there will always be some decisions which do not please every member state, or many interest groups within them. To assume that a national government can win every argument is patently absurd. Yet every single loss can, and will, be seized upon by anti-Europeans as a reason for changing the rules or even for pulling out. Their job is just too easy. Unless those who understand and care for Europe can succeed in convincing the majority of people of the validity of the bigger picture, they will lose a war of attrition.

But what is the bigger picture? If one looks behind the millions of words that have been written over the decades about the European Union and its structures and its purpose, what is the thread that pulls it all together? I believe it is quite clear and has been so from the outset. Robert Schuman and Jean Monnet set it down when, in 1950, they wrote the Schuman Declaration that was to launch the European Coal and Steel Community:

> Europe will not be made all at once, or according to a single plan. It will be built through concrete achievements which will first create a *de facto* solidarity. The coming together of the nations of Europe requires the elimination of the age-old opposition of France and Germany... *as a first stage in the federation of Europe.*

It is largely due to the failure of the political elites, at least in Britain, to face up to the logical conclusions of the process of European Union, that there is so much confusion and uncertainty today. This failure has been a major factor contributing to the mystification of the whole process and it is now time to face it openly and honestly.

Part of the Eurosceptics' strength has been based on their recognition of the gap between rhetoric and reality. Successive governments have hidden behind weasel words and claimed to have resisted the encroachment of what they dishonestly choose to call a 'federal superstate'. But it has only made their task more difficult. At least the so-called 'sceptics' were right to be sceptical about the denials and they deserve credit for having the courage to sweep away the obfuscation which, at times, has bordered on deceit. Nevertheless, they share the guilt and shame which should cling to all those who have deliberately and unashamedly sought to twist the truth about what European union means.

It is my hope that this book will help to set the record straight both by explaining the essential meaning of federalism and by showing how its application to the problems facing the European Union can help to create a new, dynamic and above all democratic Union of nations and peoples. The IGC, which is expected to complete its deliberation by the end of 1997, provides an opportunity and an agenda. I hope to provide a simple guide to the IGC that will clarify the underlying issues that need to be resolved and de-mystify the ideas and themes that are being discussed.

People whose lives will be affected by the outcome have the right to be informed and on the basis of that information to express their own ideas and aspirations. A new clarity needs to be injected into the whole debate. This time, the debate must not be reduced to irritating and ultimately irrelevant political squabbles. An opportunity must be given to people to judge the issues on their merit.

It is vital that the people themselves, and not just "Keepers of the Mystery", should be able to determine the future shape of the European Union.

2. Who's afraid of the big bad word?

Possibly the only real taboo left in society today is 'coming out' as a federalist. The usual reaction to dropping the subject casually into a conversation is either dismay or blank incomprehension. Whereas sex and religion are now acceptable as conversation topics at most tables, federalism is considered at best extremely boring and at worst deeply suspect. This might have something to do with the fact that, in England, the word itself seems vaguely dated, like the Peace Pledge Union of the 1930s or the post-war Commonwealth Party. It suggests earnest meetings in dusty town halls or pamphlets being composed on old-fashioned typewriters perched on deeply lined wooden desks – an example of well-meaning English intellectual eccentricity.

According to another view of federalism common in some parts of the world, most notably in parts of rural North America, federalists, at least of the international variety, have become, along with the United Nations, a symbol of an evil conspiracy engaged in a quest for world domination, aiming to enslave God-fearing, gun carrying, communist-hating survivalists.

It would seem difficult to square the two images; yet I suspect they have become fused in the minds of some of the more virulent Euro-phobes. The idea that cells of usually rather conventionally turned out middle-aged men and women together with a few students, both conservative and radical, are plotting with fanatical Brussels-based technocrats to impose a European super-state upon unsuspecting European citizens has a certain charm, but it says more about latent paranoia than any political reality.

The fact is that the numbers of open supporters of European or world federalism in the UK have declined dramatically from their peak in the late 1930s to a handful of adherents today. This is a pity, but the trend is showing important signs of being reversed. Not only is there a growing understanding and enthusiasm among young people about the possibilities it offers for open, responsive and democratic European government, many of the principles inherent in federalism are actually becoming incorporated into modern business strategy.

At a time when ideologies are being universally abandoned, federalism has the advantage of being an anti-ideological political theory. It is essentially a system in which power and decision-making are divided and balanced between different, appropriate levels of government all of which must be made as accountable as possible to the citizens. Its aim is the maximum empowerment of the citizen at every level of government. It recognises that people express their political and economic needs and aspirations at a variety of different levels from the local community, through regions and nation states up to, and including, international institutions. It offers a way to balance and reconcile the vitality of the local community with the growing recognition that security, trade and the environment require institutionalised international cooperation. The key is to determine at which level decisions should be taken and powers allocated and how best citizens, acting both individually and collectively, can exercise democratic control.

What federalism most emphatically is not is an attempt to impose a centralised, bureaucratic and unaccountable super-state upon unwilling and resentful nation states. It is this perception of federalism, used even by many who should know better, that has poisoned the debate in Britain about Europe's future, created confusion in the public's mind about our continental partners' objectives and frightened many pro-Europeans away from putting their heads above the parapet. Federalism is a system which aims to balance both centralising and decentralising tendencies but, as Ferdinand Mount points out in *The British Constitution Now*: "There is all the difference in the world between a voluntary and a coerced federation."

Despite being called 'Federations', Yugoslavia and the Soviet Union were artificial creations held together by the force of Communist totalitarianism. The failure of these artificial states to hold together after the controlling powers lost their authority did not undermine the validity of federalism but did illustrate the fondness dictatorships often display for misusing language. As Ferdinand Mount notes:

> [The] distinction between a federation which permits secession and one which doesn't is not only all important to unhappy citizens of member-states in coerced federations such as Yugoslavia and the Soviet Union; it also suggests that sovereignty may be reserved, even by members of a federation. To put it bluntly, if you go in voluntarily, well aware that you can get out again if you don't like it, can you be said to have ceded sovereignty?

The difference between a voluntary federation from which a country can secede and one into which it has been coerced is fundamental. But it also illustrates beautifully that like Humpty Dumpty, who gave words the meanings he chose, it has been in the nature of totalitarian, especially communist, regimes to use words like 'democratic' and 'federalist' when they meant nothing of the sort. But, if such misuse does not remove democracy from everyday usage, why should it disqualify federalism?

In the *Encyclopædia Britannica*, federalism is defined as:

> the mode of political organisation that unites separate polities within an overarching political system in such a way as to allow each to maintain its own fundamental political integrity. Federal systems do this by requiring that basic policies be made and implemented through negotiation in some form, so that all the members can share in making and executing decisions.

So much for imposing power and authority upon unwilling participants! The *Britannica* continues by explaining that the principles of federalism "stress the virtues of dispersed power centres as a means for safeguarding individual and local liberties".

If we look more closely at this definition, what does it suggest are the key characteristics of federal government? Firstly, the need for each part of the system to maintain its political integrity – hardly a recipe for a centralised super-state. Secondly, the need for decisions to be made through negotiation – a more prosaic way of describing Winston Churchill's preference for "jaw-jaw rather than war-war". And thirdly, the safeguarding of individual and local liberties – possibly the most crucial requirement in an age in which not just governments but some corporations seem prepared to undermine many of the basic rights and freedoms of the individual.

This, of course, is the theory and it would be foolish to pretend that federal systems have developed in the same way wherever they have been used. The sheer number and diversity of states which have adopted federal systems make that impossible. Conditions prevailing in the United States of America at the time of the drafting of the United States Constitution were clearly not the same as in post-war Germany or at the time of India's independence. But many of the same arguments and principles apply. For example, there is an extraordinary vitality in the *Federalist Papers*, through which the principles and structures upon which a future American government would be based were vigorously debated, which reflect some of the current debate over the future of the European Union. The authors of the *Federalist Papers*, Alexander Hamilton, James Madison and John Jay, confronted the same type of problems that face the builders of today's European Union: what powers should be exercised at what level of government? To what degree should a constitution place symmetry and theory above expediency and practical political reality? What are the rights and duties of citizens and to whom are their main loyalties given?

The German federal constitution, although a substantially different document from the American constitution, was nevertheless designed to answer similar questions, including the need to seek a balance between the power and authority of the federal government and that of the *Länder*, the constituent German states which have their own individual and distinctive history and traditions. One of the reasons why the Germans have understood European federalism has been that they have grown to understand its potential for guaranteeing both democratic rights and a balance between central and local government.

Ironically, the German constitution was heavily influenced by British thinkers and administrators during the allied occupation of Germany in the aftermath of the war. Discussing prewar ideas of European Union in *Eminent Europeans*, John Pinder notes that one of the oddities of the history of West European integration is that so many of the early prophets of an integrated Europe came from outside the six states which constituted its core: from the successor states of the Austro-Hungarian empire, from Switzerland and from England. It was a British writer and statesman, Lord Lothian, who was to convert to the cause the most dynamic of the post-war European federalists – Altiero Spinelli – who had read Lothian's works while imprisoned by Mussolini for his anti-fascist activities on the island of Ventotene.

In the nineteenth century, the constitutional expert Dicey rejected the federalist approach as an answer to the Irish question as unconstitutional. For all the later British input to federalist thought, Britain's application of federalism has been confined to former colonies and defeated enemies. Dicey's view, which has underlain most opposition to federalism in this country ever since, is that it undermines the sovereignty of Parliament or, as it is constitutionally defined – "The Queen in Parliament". Whether or not sovereignty should be held by Parliament in quite such an unfettered way is debatable: what is clear is that in the context of Britain's membership of international organisations, including the North Atlantic Treaty Organisation and the European Union, it is now largely illusory. That 650 elected men and women sitting in one chamber and over eleven hundred hereditary and appointed peers in the other should deem themselves to be the sole manifestation of the will of the British people on every political, social and economic matter facing the country today and in the future is not just wrong but manifestly absurd.

At base, it is the British people who must be sovereign and free to express their sovereignty at whichever level of government they deem to be the most satisfactory and effective. Federalism offers them this opportunity at both the national and at the international level.

The author and business philosopher Professor Charles Handy made the clearest contemporary account of federal principles in *The Independent* in February 1995. Professor Handy began by observing that:

> Federalism is not a system of imposed uniformity, nor is it just an alliance of common interests; it offers, rather, as much variety as possible and as much uniformity as is helpful in order to give the different interests some common force. The devil is in the detail of federalism, not its principle. If we throw out the principle because we do not like the detail, we are depriving ourselves of one of the best ways of handling complexity in organisations. Business after business is, in fact, inching its way towards federalism, without always appreciating that that is what is happening, as they seek to find ways to be big and uniform in some respects, but small, local and different in others; to give people and groups their head, but yet to bind them together.

Professor Handy proceeds by identifying five principles in federalism that makes it suitable both for business and government. The first is **'subsidiarity'** which, as he points out, was not invented by Jacques Delors or the Maastricht negotiators but, in fact, comes from an old term in German theology turned into a moral axiom centuries ago by the Catholic Church. A more recent papal encyclical from 1941 described it thus: "It is a grave evil and a disturbance of the right order for a larger and higher organisation to arrogate to itself functions which can be performed efficiently by smaller and lower bodies." Professor Handy puts it more simply:

> Stealing other peoples' decisions is wrong: yet managers do it all the time, in the name of efficiency, as do governments who turn their people into dependents, or parents who cannot bear to see their children take the wrong decision. In organisations, as in the European Union, subsidiarity means a sort of reverse delegation whereby the centre does only what the parts agree that it should do, because it is in all their interests for some things to be done collectively or uniformly. What these things are has to be a matter for negotiation between the partners for federalism is, and always has to be, a negotiated settlement, not an imposed one.

The second principle Professor Handy identifies is that of **twin citizenship**, pointing out that it is perfectly possible to be a citizen at several levels. A Bavarian is also a German, just as a Texan is an American. Similarly, Scots and Welsh people have loyalties to both their own nation and to the UK. As Professor Handy points out:

> In organisations it is important to realise that one owes something not only to one's immediate group or subsidiary, but also to the larger whole, which means that, occasionally, the immediate interests of the smaller unit must be sacrificed to the interests of the whole for the ultimate benefit of all.

The third principle is that of **interdependence** – the glue which binds the federation. In Professor Handy's words:

> The smaller parts must not be dependent only on the centre, because that tilts the balance of power too much one way. Federalism, therefore, counsels that the necessary centres of excellence, or leadership roles, are spread among the partners, just as the various European institutions are spread among the member countries.

The task of the centre should be to facilitate as much as to act or deliver the goods itself.

The fourth principle Professor Handy suggests is, **a common law** "[that] ensures that all parties to the federation work to a common set of rules and standards in all things that really matter". This can apply to a whole range of political and economic activity from the single market to information systems to a common currency. But, as Professor Handy points out, whereas convergence criteria are not necessary for a common information system, they have to be created if a common currency is to work and "that means, ultimately, transferring payments from the richer to the poorer. The pull of twin citizenship would have to be very strong to withstand the strain of such generosity."

Whether or not such transfers of wealth are, in fact, offset by the overall generation of higher levels of prosperity and new trading opportunities will be examined later on but the point Professor Handy makes is a crucial one: the European Community has always accepted that the rights accorded to the member states must be balanced by their responsibilities to the poorer, often peripheral, regions, that may not automatically share in the prosperity that has been generated in the more central regions. It is a policy from which an increasing number of UK regions have benefited in recent years.

The fifth and final point made by Professor Handy is fundamental to all expressions of federalism throughout the world – **the separation of powers** – and seen most clearly in the American Constitution. Unlike the British Parliament, which jealously guards its powers of legislation and ultimate executive control (though both have been undermined by the determination of government to force its will upon Parliament through the power of the Whips), federations have always sought ways to divide and distribute powers between different institutions. Similarly in the European Union, legislative, executive and judicial powers are exercised in a variety of combinations by the five main institutions: the European Council, the Council of Ministers, the European Parliament, the Commission and the Court of Justice.

In Professor Handy's words: "A separation of powers makes life more difficult for those in charge, but it does spread the power around and thus protect one from a bad dictator or a mischievous oligarchy. Federalism has always seen itself as the antidote to any undue concentration of power." Indeed, even with all the most modern means of communication available, it is almost impossible to envisage a single individual or even a political group able to dominate the European Union in the way that individual countries have been dominated. Added to that, the inability of rhetoric to cross the cultural divides would substantially reduce its emotive force.

In his conclusion, Professor Handy suggests that:

> Federalism is neither good nor bad in itself. It is an
> entirely appropriate form of government for our times
> – times which require large agglomerations of re-
> sources for some purposes but which also want local

> variety, and as much local autonomy as possible ... It
> would be more pleasing if we stopped calling it names
> and got on with applying the principles, because whether
> we realise it or not, we are walking that way, but it is
> never sensible to walk backwards into the future.

This cannot be bettered as a summary of our present predicament, yet I believe that there is a sixth important benefit of federalism which should be stated: it imposes upon ordinary citizens the need to **take their political responsibilies more seriously**. While most governments seem to do everything possible to avoid public debate about contentious issues, it is also true that many citizens believe that the democratic process consists of merely casting a vote in the ballot box every few years and then complaining about the result.

Curiously, while bookshops, especially at airports and railways stations, are filled with books suggesting that the key to success in everything from sex to business requires the individual to take full responsibility for his or her decisions, there is virtually no literature urging the same for political responsibility. And yet if we want government, at whatever level, to carry out our wishes, it is our responsibility both to say what we want and to shout loudly if our wishes are ignored without adequate explanation.

It is a universal phenomenon that people moan at politicians but do little to activate a change. The American writer and philosopher, Henry Thoreau, wrote: "Must the citizen ever for a moment, or in the least degree, resign his conscience to the legislator? Why has every man a conscience then? I think we should be men first and subjects afterwards." The point is taken up by Andrew Marr in *Ruling Britannia*:

> If power has shifted away from politicians to markets
> and bureaucrats, so that things that are central to our
> lives – the cost of money, the availability of work, the
> regulations that govern our leisure and our country-
> side – are decided without political discussion, plenty
> of people will be unworried by that. It could be called
> the final victory of paternalism and liberalism over
> politics. A world in which the awkward machinery of

> ballot boxes, parties and parliaments can be allowed
> to dwindle into unimportance. Shop, don't vote: you get
> more choice, you have more control and the makers of
> commodities lie less often than the makers of laws.

And Simon Jenkins in *Accountable To None* makes a similar point:

> Democratic politics is endangered where the 'habit of
> association' is allowed, indeed encouraged, to degener-
> ate. Citizenship is not a matter of exercising consumer
> choice of products and services where permitted and
> voting once every four or five years. The ceaseless exer-
> cise of political freedom is not just a right: it is an obli-
> gation on every member of a sophisticated community.

Of course, the problem is not just confined to Britain or, indeed, to
Europe. All governments are finding it increasingly difficult to govern. Electorates, bombarded daily with information, opinions and,
not infrequently, misinformation, by ever more powerful press and
media interests, are growing cynical and impatient with politicians.
And if people are increasingly mistrustful of their national political
establishments, it is not surprising that they will be even more sus-
picious of institutions, bureaucrats and politicians about whom they
know little, operating at an international level.

It is in dealing with this growing sense of alienation, however, that
a channel of agreement opens up between Sir James Goldsmith's
arguments on the one hand and those of many European reformers
on the other. Indeed, without wishing to insult him, some of his
suggestions would appear to be almost federalist! When he calls in
The Trap for democracy to be participatory and not just representative, meaning that citizens should retain the final decision on matters which will significantly affect their society, he speaks for many
who see within such a suggestion, the spirit of subsidiarity. I would
go further and support his call for an extension of the principle of
local referenda as operated in Switzerland where a petition signed
by 50,000 people can insist that proposals presented to Parliament
be submitted to a public referendum. As Andrew Marr points out,
"Swiss go to the polls more times in one year than most Europeans

in a lifetime." It is a principle that appears to conform with Aristotle's belief that "They [the citizens] have the fullest sovereign power."

In some respects, the newest members of the EU – Austria, Finland and Sweden – are the best informed because their recent entry into the Union depended upon a positive outcome in referenda in which the issues were widely discussed. Similarly, in France, Denmark and Ireland, which all held referenda following the Maastricht Treaty, not only were governments forced to circulate information but there was also an opportunity for people to air deep-seated uncertainties and frustrations and demand answers to their questions.

Such a process has not happened in the UK since 1975 when, by a significant margin of two to one, the British people responded positively to being asked whether they wished to remain in the European Economic Community (EEC). This result might have settled the matter for once and for all, except for a suspicion that the real nature of the what was being agreed was not fully understood. The arguments in favour of membership rested primarily upon the economic and trade benefits that would accrue from belonging to a free trade area and the disadvantages that might follow from exclusion. It has become increasingly clear that many, if not most, people believed that the referendum was about Britain's membership of a common market, not a political union. Even if they were explained, the political implications of membership were certainly not emphasised and it is unlikely that they were widely understood at the time.

This was no small misunderstanding. As citizens of the member states have watched what they believe to be national decisions move into a European orbit, bewilderment has turned into suspicion and then anger. Although this anger must not be exaggerated – many people are as much concerned about whether a decision is a good or a bad one as to the level at which it is taken – it is crucial that, as we approach the next IGC, the full picture is given.

The sense of confusion is exacerbated by the fact that the IGC is happening at a time when, in Will Hutton's words: "British institutions, burnished with age old legitimacy and once seen as impregnable, are cracking under the pressure as pretension meets reality."

The European Union is part of that reality and our membership has drawn attention to the inadequacy of many of our existing governmental institutions. And, by so doing, appears to undermine them.

It is not surprising, therefore, that many MPs who cling to the idea that sovereignty in Britain rests with the Crown in Parliament find Europe a threat when it so clearly illustrates the limits of their powers. Their wings have already been clipped by government and they are frightened of losing what powers they still have. The uncomfortable fact is that the power of elected representatives of the people at every level – local, regional and national – has been diminished in favour of central governmental power. One of the greatest political changes in the 1980s was the transfer of powers from local authorities to national government, yet the government refused to yield power to European co-decision.

The antidote is a closer examination of the merits of the federal solution, undertaken with an open mind. Within it lie the seeds of a new relationship, not just between Britain and Europe but between every level of British government. It is, I believe, the way to restore sovereignty to the British people.

The time is now right, in the light of the current IGC, to consider the fundamental structure of the government of Western Europe, and the role that federalism has to play in it. But this IGC is not taking place in a vacuum – it is a stage in a process of European integration that has been taking place for fifty years, and the questions we must consider are inextricably bound up in both the structure of the European Union and the developments taking place in the world around it.

3. Certainties, risks and challenges

The collapse of Communism and the demise of the Soviet Union may have made Western Europe a safer place; but it is less certain than it was a decade ago. Then, provided that the balance of power (or terror) could avert war, there was a certain simplicity, at least for western Europeans, about living in a world of two superpowers. It encouraged a feeling of solidarity, spurred the process of post-war economic recovery and, by contrast with totalitarian regimes to the east, reaffirmed most citizens' belief in the democratic process of the West.

Today, there are no such certainties. Four major events are sharply changing the world in which we live and are raising new questions to which there seem to be no definitive answers.

The first two – the collapse of communist regimes in Russia and East-Central Europe and the subsequent re-unification of Germany – are intimately related. They have obvious implications for defence and security, but also raise issues concerning our own systems of government. The question of enlargement of the club of western European nations continues to play a major part both in the growing demand for reform of western European governments and also in the way that the European Union is looking to reshape its institutions.

Six countries signed the first treaties creating the European Community. There are now fifteen members of the European Union (EU), as it is now called, and in five years the figure may have reached twenty, with a further ten European nations still hoping to join. At the same time, Germany, a defeated and impoverished nation fifty years ago, has become the largest and most economically powerful nation on the continent and, what is more, that generation which, in reaction to defeat and occupation, inspired the German commitment to building a united Europe will soon have passed on

By themselves these alone would be profound changes, but they are perhaps less important than two further changes: the shift of economic power and growth from the West to the dynamic economies of the Pacific Rim, in particular China; and the ever-accelerating technological and information revolution. While this latter is perhaps a cliché, it is one whose profound implications for the world economy have yet to be fully realised.

With growth rates far outstripping Europe's, the 'economic tigers' of the Pacific Rim not only challenge Europe's economy but also its political and cultural influence. Europe's imperial heritage has carried it through much of this century but will count for very little in the next millennium. At the same time, with billions of pounds, dollars, yen and deutschmarks metaphorically racing daily around the planet and multinational corporations able to shift production and personnel from one continent to another in the search for maximum profitability, it is debatable whether any government has much control over its national economy. In Will Hutton's description in *The State We're In*:

> Capital can now flow freely within the EU and between Europe, Japan and North America. The flows have grown exponentially. In 1992, for example, the stock of international bank assets was more than double the volume of world trade; thirty years earlier they were only fractionally more than 10% of world trade. Trading in currencies takes place 24 hours a day.

As journalist and author Anthony Sampson pointed out in article in *The Independent*:

> The huge flow of foreign funds ... tests the integrity of every institution to the limit. In the global context, national politicians or administrators begin to look more like local councillors confronting big-time developers. The European national institutions at the

end of the 20th century look embarrassingly like the American state legislatures at the end of the 19th when they faced the power of the great continental trusts such as Standard Oil or the railroads that brought the state politicians onto the payroll. The United States, unlike Europe today, already had a federal government in place; but it was not until the Thirties that it became an effective regulator for inter-state commerce and caught up with the scale of finance and industry ... That kind of authority is still a long way off for today's Europe. Meanwhile, global money and power are moving faster out of control.

This is the context in which politicians and civil servants have to try to formulate ideas for the future of the European Union during the coming months. The current Intergovernmental Conference (IGC) faces an even greater set of complex choices than those in the run-up to Maastricht. There is a danger that it will result in another legalistic and confused document which is then bulldozed through national parliaments without adequate explanation or popular support. For the IGC to go down that path and spawn another Maastricht would be intolerable. To assume that it would be automatically acceptable to all European citizens would be both naive and dangerous for the whole course of European integration.

This time, it is vital to ensure proper debate with widespread participation. As the dust of Maastricht settles and if Europe does move towards both economic and monetary union and further enlargement, the political as well as economic implications will be profound. Fundamental decisions about the kind of society we are trying to build and its core values will be taken increasingly at a European level. For example, the historic debate between political 'left' and political 'right' will be argued out increasingly on the European stage. National governments will cease to have in their control some of the traditional methods, like exchange and interest rate manipulation, including devaluation, that have been used in the past to cushion potential economic crises.

Europe has for too long been thought of as a 'mystery', a hard and boring story rendered even more unapproachable by the endless use of jargon and acronyms. Don't let that put you off! If you have found it difficult to grasp what has been happening, you are certainly not alone. Anyone listening to the debates on Europe in the House of Commons will have been amazed to discover the extraordinarily low level of knowledge and information even among MPs. And if MPs are ill-informed, it is hardly surprising that voters are confused and uncertain.

And yet, the European story is not such a difficult one to tell. Admittedly, it has no identifiable start and the end may never be reached. Part of the problem for many people in understanding what is happening is that the European Union is not a finished product but an evolving process. But it has an exciting enough narrative and characters who have earned their place in history. Indeed, if it were portrayed as a story, it might be possible to rekindle an interest in many people who have been thoroughly bored by a debate that seems to sink ever more deeply into a swamp of unrelated slogans, details and statistics.

The first step is to throw out all the 'Eurospeak', the technical and legal jargon that characterises much writing about Europe. For most people, it is not only confusing and irrelevant but actually conceals what should be essentially choices about values. And the second is to follow the story not just as a passive reader but as a participant in an interactive narrative. Up to now, the plot and the characters have been determined by a small group of authors: the politicians and bureaucrats. The time has come for the readers – the electors and citizens – to take it over and choose for themselves the path to take.

It is said that there are only seven jokes in the world which are endlessly recycled. In much the same way the entire debate about the future of the European Union can be boiled down to a dozen or so points of fundamental principle.

Ironically, at a time when no-one in the main political parties wants to re-open too many contentious issues, they will all be raised in one form or another, either overtly or by implication, at the IGC, since they lie at the heart of the question of where Europe is going. How they are resolved will determine the nature of the European Union for the next generation.

Because, at heart, they are as much about values as facts, these issues are not difficult to understand. But it is vital for the future health of the European Union that they are understood and widely debated throughout the member states.

The **first** is the question of how power and decision-making is divided between the European institutions and the member states. What is at stake is the balance of power between the interests of the Community as a whole and the member states individually. Although it is at the heart of the debate about the future of the Union, it is unlikely ever to be fully resolved.

The **second** is the balance between the institutions. Should the European Parliament (EP), as the only directly elected European institution, have the right to share all decisions with the Council of Ministers or should power remain fundamentally with the representatives of the member states? This issue concerns the democratic legitimacy of the European Union as a whole. Defenders of national sovereignty will favour the preservation of the rights of the member states while those who wish to see greater integration will favour the Union.

The **third** is the role of the Commission. Should its wings be clipped by reducing its role to that of a civil service or should it be seen as the embryo of a future European government? If the former, then it is likely that the impetus to ever-closer Union will be lost. If the latter, then Europe may move inexorably towards a federal system of government, whether of a parliamentary or presidential model. Or, perhaps, the present structure could simply be reformed so as to narrow but strengthen the focus of the Commission's activities.

The **fourth** is whether all member states should march together towards a common goal or whether different speeds and objectives are acceptable. Some will argue strongly that those members who do not wish to move forward at the same speed as the leaders should not be entitled to block those that do. This is essentially about the use of the veto in the Council of Ministers which can be used by member states to block decisions they believe would be against their fundamental national interest. Ironically, part of the debate will be about whether the result of the IGC itself should have to receive unanimous support in order to come into force.

The **fifth** concerns the budget, most especially, the Common Agricultural Policy (CAP) and the cohesion funds. Although the CAP is not on the agenda, it takes up about half the Union's budget and, in its present form, makes further enlargement almost impossible. Its reform, though widely recognised as necessary, would mean confronting the farmers, who are a powerful lobby in many member states, with a potentially severe electoral price. Equally sensitive are the cohesion funds, which require the movement of funds from richer to poorer countries and regions, and take up nearly a third of the Community's budget. Both will affect the speed and timing of enlargement.

The **sixth** is maintaining a level playing field between the member states for companies and individuals in the single market. Covering everything from the harmonisation of standards to the acceptability of subsidies, this is one of the key issues that defines how widely the Community's powers should extend into the way member states legislate. Where does the 'market' that needs to be harmonised end and those aspects of our lives we want to keep separate begin?

The **seventh** – the social dimension and the rights of the work force – concerns the issue of international competitiveness. Is a progressive social policy the prerequisite of a civilised society or will it merely make Europe uncompetitive? It is an argument at the centre of the debate in the UK between the government and the opposition parties.

The **eighth** is the meaning of European citizenship and its scope and implications. How far should the rights of European citizens be extended, and are there also related duties and responsibilities? How far is European public opinion prepared to accept the idea of a European citizenship that exists in addition to citizenship at the national level?

The **ninth** is about openness and accountability. Is it time for Europe to move towards a more open form of government, perhaps modelled on Scandinavian lines, or will decisions continue to be taken in secret by the Council of Ministers with issues such as the management of Justice and Home Affairs never facing proper democratic scrutiny?

The **tenth** is the role of the European Union in the world and to what degree all the key issues of defence, security, foreign affairs and external economic affairs should be taken at the European or the national level. This is obviously related to the first and second points but has the added dimension of international relations and external pressures.

The **eleventh** is economic and monetary union. Will the economic criteria for convergence in the Maastricht Treaty be realised by enough member states to go forward? If they are not met, will the whole idea collapse? Is there sufficient political will to press ahead regardless, either immediately or in the future? Although, like enlargement, this will not be directly on the agenda, it will determine, possibly more than any other issue, the speed and depth of future European integration addressed in the IGC.

The **twelfth** and final point is further enlargement. This could prove expensive and difficult, but so would the alternative – an unstable and insecure Europe. Like economic and monetary union, enlargement affects all the preceding issues and will change forever the nature of the process of integration. A Union of thirty nations would not only alter the internal dynamics of the Union itself but would have a profound effect on the rest of the world.

This then is a book about these choices. It outlines and examines them in the hope that they may stimulate public debate before decisions are taken. The future success of the European Union depends upon electors and citizens knowing what it is all about.

The purpose of this book is not to seek to answer all the questions that will be raised but to ask them ahead of time, and to provide a conceptual framework into which they can fit, so that, at last, a serious debate can take place. It is not an academic book. Indeed, I shall try and do everything to avoid jargon and undue complexity wherever possible. In a book of this size, a vast amount of information will have to be left out. That is both deliberate and surprisingly difficult: I have avoided the temptation to cram in as many facts as possible, preferring to consider issues and arguments.

Chapters 4 and 5 contain a brief account of the history and development of the European Union, chapter 6 describes the key institutions, chapters 7 to 14 examine the main issues facing the IGC, chapters 15 and 16 provide a brief account of economic and monetary union and the future enlargement of the Union, and chapter 17 presents a federalist solution to many of the problems raised.

The European Union must have a relationship not just with governments, or even regions, but with people and their communities, if it is to mean anything. Like other forms of government, it needs 're-inventing' in such a way that it reflects rather than dominates peoples needs and wishes. The European Union must, above all, recognise that its legitimacy depends upon its whole-hearted acceptance by the people of Europe. In as much as change will come, it must come from the bottom up and not the other way around. To their credit, many of the key players within the Union already recognise the crucial importance of winning the trust of the people they serve. I hope that this book helps to develop and extend this trust by offering some basic and simple information to enable you, the reader, to make up your mind about the values involved in the great debate. This book aims to help you make political choices about Europe and your future.

4. From the Second World War to the Single Market

The idea of a united Europe is certainly not a new one. It has been advocated by political thinkers and practical politicians as a remedy to a thousand years of fratricidal and bloody disputes between European nations. But it was only after the unparalleled catastrophe of two world wars, which caused over 40 million deaths, that the first practical steps were taken towards building a united Europe.

Until relatively modern times, Europe was widely perceived as a cultural entity permitting the relatively free movement of scholars, artists and traders. The Roman Empire, which covered much of what we now know as Western Europe, had brought to a largely tribal continent universal laws, a common language for the educated elite and a degree of economic interdependence. By the time of its demise, Christianity, although divided between Roman Catholicism and Eastern Orthodoxy, was fast becoming the common religion of Europe.

When Charlemagne was crowned Emperor by the Pope on Christmas Day 800 AD, his empire bore a remarkable resemblance to the territory covered by the original six members of the European Community. In the Middle Ages, Europe was known as 'Christendom' and became the target for conquest by many who sought to unite it by a mixture of diplomacy and force of arms. Others tried the force of reason: a number of thinkers as varied as the Duc de Sully, William Penn, Leibnitz, Montesquieu, Kant and, in more modern times, Lord Lothian, Lord Beveridge, Barbara Wootton and Lionel Robbins advocated some form of a united Europe as a way to preserve peace for posterity. Lothian especially devoted much of his life to searching for a solution to war. Andrea Bosco in an essay in *The Larger Idea*, writes:

> Observing that war is the most permanent feature in international relations, Lothian isolated in the 'division of humanity into absolute separate states' the 'mechanical causes' of war ... All men and women of goodwill are interested in the problem of peace and nobody believes in war itself, because death is the negation of life but 'that sentiment only extends to the sociological or humanitarian field, when you turn to politics, it disappears.'

Hopes were invested in the creation of the League of Nations but they were frustrated when, with few restrictions placed by it on the exercise of unfettered national sovereignty and no authority or mechanism to enforce its decisions, it collapsed in the face of Fascist and Nazi aggression. Jean Monnet claimed that the scales dropped from his eyes when the League failed to stop Japan annexing Manchuria in 1932. François Duchêne has argued that "Monnet considered the League of Nations to be powerless because every country had a veto on decisions."

Largely because of the failure of the League of Nations, Monnet recognised that the permanent preservation of peace in Europe would require the pooling of some areas of national sovereignty for the greater good. Fortunately, he was not alone. Just as American political genius was released by the American revolution in the late eighteenth century, Europe was blessed, in the immediate post-war period, with statesmen in many countries who possessed the vision, ability and political skill to rebuild the devastated continent. Jean Monnet and Robert Schuman in France, Alcide De Gasperi in Italy, Konrad Adenauer in Germany, Paul-Henri Spaak in Belgium and, although he was to hold ambivalent opinions about Britain's role, Winston Churchill. These were the outstanding examples of those recognised today as the 'founding fathers' of Europe. Extraordinarily different characters from very different political and ideological traditions, they shared a common vision of a united Europe able to guarantee its citizens the holy grail of long term peace.

The Congress of Europe, held in the Hague in 1948, was attended by, among others, representatives of resistance movements who had discovered a sense of shared purpose in their opposition to Nazi and Fascist occupation and was concerned to foster reconciliation between former enemies by committing itself to the economic, political and cultural union of Europe. It took three practical steps.

First, it established the Council of Europe, whose Assembly is open to representatives from the parliaments of all the democratic European states and which has 39 members at present. A forum for discussing all matters of common European importance and social issues, the Council of Europe can only make recommendations to governments. Since 1989, its scope has expanded to include some of the new democracies of Central and Eastern Europe and the former Soviet Union including, since the beginning of 1996, the Russian Federation. Although all the member states of the European Union are members of the Council of Europe, they are totally independent institutions. The European flag, whose twelve stars have often been thought, mistakenly, to represent the member states of the Union when it had twelve members, actually originated at the Council of Europe.

Secondly, the Congress initiated the drafting of a European Convention on Human Rights, backed by a Court of Human Rights. Most European countries in the Council have incorporated the Convention into their laws; the UK has not, but it does recognise the Court as a final court of appeal. Recently, some of the Court's judgements, for example enforcing equal access for men and women over 60 to reduced fares on public transport and the ruling against the British government over the IRA killings in Gibraltar, have hit the headlines.

Finally, the Congress set up the European Movement as a 'people to people' voluntary organisation to bring about economic, monetary and political union in Europe.

The mood of the Congress of Europe was predominantly federalist. It offered an occasion for reconciliation and for emotion. It was as if the high tone of idealism that runs through the speeches and poems delivered in the great medieval hall in the Hague where the meeting was convened embodied a cathartic reaction to the pent up pain and trauma of six years of total war. On reading the speeches that were made by contributors as diverse as Winston Churchill, Duncan

Sandys, Denis de Rougemont, Paul Ramadier and Salvador de Madariaga, it is hard to square the extraordinary sense of purpose and conviction about the future of Europe with some of the more cynical and banal reactions in evidence today. It is also interesting to note the size and importance of the British delegation which, as well as those previously mentioned, also included Adrian Boult and the then Poet Laureate, John Masefield.

In retrospect, we are lucky that the work to rebuild Europe did not end there. Nor, thankfully, did it rely on the emotion of the time to carry it through more sceptical times.

Instead, French Foreign Minister Robert Schuman and Jean Monnet, whose career had included being Deputy Secretary-General of the League of Nations and a war-time adviser to both Winston Churchill and Franklin Roosevelt, proposed a revolutionary scheme to bind together those countries that had been at the centre of the conflict in both world wars – France and Germany – in a common framework for the production and distribution of coal and steel. Instead of re-kindling the spirit of revenge that had led from the Treaty of Versailles, at the end of the First World War, to further conflict less than a generation later, a new strategy was sought that would tie the former enemies so closely that future wars would become impractical. The key ideas underlying the building of modern Europe were outlined in the Schuman Declaration of 1950:

> Europe will not be made all at once, or according to a single plan. It will be built through concrete achievements which will first create a *de facto* solidarity. The coming together of the nations of Europe requires the elimination of the age-old opposition of France and Germany...

> The pooling of coal and steel production should immediately provide for the setting up of common foundations for economic development as a first step in the federation of Europe, and will change the destinies of those regions which have long been devoted to the manufacture of munitions of war, of which they have been the most constant victims.

Such ideas encapsulated the philosophy behind the foundation in 1952 of the European Coal and Steel Community (ECSC) which began with an initial membership of six – France, Germany, Italy and the Benelux countries. As can be seen from this extract, federalism was not an afterthought but the central purpose of the Coal and Steel Community from the outset. For the first time in their history, national governments agreed to delegate part of their sovereignty, albeit in limited, clearly defined matters, to a High Authority consisting of persons chosen by them but acting independently and collectively enjoying powers to take decisions in the common interest of the member states.

The UK, although invited to join, declined to do so believing, wrongly as it turned out, that the project was unlikely to succeed.

When the creation of a European Defence Community and a Political Community, designed to move the Six swiftly to full Union, failed in 1954 because of opposition from the French Parliament, the initiative was switched from the political field to towards greater economic integration. For many of the early proponents of European union, the failure of the plans for a Political Community was a bitter blow. It marked the end of the first full-blown period of postwar idealism and showed the limitations of relying solely upon the spirit of reconciliation. It did not, however, daunt Monnet who had long recognised that success would come from gradual change based upon finding areas of common interest that did not arouse popular mistrust. It also confirmed his belief in the importance of setting a goal and moving forward in stages.

The next stage came on 25 March 1957, when the six members of the Coal and Steel Community took a major step towards economic integration by signing the Treaties of Rome which created the European Economic Community (EEC), commonly known as the Common Market, and the European Atomic Energy Community (EURATOM), which pooled the peaceful development of atomic energy.

The main objective of the European Economic Community was to move towards the free movement throughout the Community of goods, persons, services and capital. In an attempt to achieve this it established a customs union by dismantling all quotas and tariff barriers to internal trade while establishing a common external tariff for goods imported from third countries.

The Treaty also provided for common policies on:

- **agriculture**: the Common Agricultural Policy, which subsequently set up price support systems for farmers in order to boost their production and incomes;
- **transport** and **competition**;
- **external trade**;
- the **harmonisation** of legislation.

The EEC was always meant to be more than just a customs union. Membership of the EEC meant a commitment to the free movement of both capital and labour, the right to set up businesses in other member states, and the coordination and rationalisation of social welfare goals.

To assist in these aims, three structures were established: the European Social Fund to develop employment opportunities for workers and boost their standard of living, the European Investment Bank to further economic expansion through loans and guarantees, and a European Development Fund to help former and existing colonies. There were also escape clauses within the Treaty which permitted divergence in national policy should a state decide it was necessary on the grounds of national security.

The Treaty (as amended by the 1965 Merger Treaty) also set up the common institutions of the three Communities:

- the Commission;
- the Parliament (originally composed of members of national parliaments);
- the Council of Ministers;
- the Court of Justice.

The role of institutions was one of Monnet's recurring themes. He believed that progress required the legitimacy and continuity which democratic institutions lent to human endeavour. In the words of the Swiss philosopher, Henri-Frédéric Amiel: "Each man's experience starts again from the beginning. Only institutions grow wiser: they accumulate collective experience; and, owing to this experience and this wisdom, men subject to the same rules will not see their own nature changing, but their behaviour gradually transformed."

It is interesting to juxtapose this belief in the importance of institutions with modern scepticism towards all bureaucracies; attacks are made constantly against the Brussels 'Eurocracy' yet behaviour throughout the Union has been gradually transformed. Regulations emanating from European institutions may frequently be resented but usually no more than any other legislation. Even in Britain, where much of the press and media delights in exposing each and every European legislative absurdity, whether true or false, people are more concerned whether the legislation is good or bad than where it came from. Whether such tolerance is being stretched too far, however, is now central to the debate on the Union's future.

The Treaty of Rome was also explicit in its commitment to eventual Economic and Political Union. At the time, successive British governments still believed that Britain had a unique role in the world at the point where three circles of influence were perceived to meet: the Atlantic relationship, the Commonwealth and Europe. Britain was prepared to form the much looser European Free Trade Association (EFTA) with the Scandinavian countries, Austria, Portugal and Switzerland, but felt she could stay outside the EEC.

This soon proved to be a major miscalculation. As Lord Howe has subsequently suggested: "The UK was only one of five medium sized European nations and by no means the most successful or influential in continental politics. America was not convinced of the importance of the special relationship." Indeed, American administrations have consistently supported the process of European integration both as a means of rationalising and stabilising European politics and in order to disentangle themselves from an increasingly unwelcome financial burden. A richer Europe could be expected to pay more for its own defence.

It was also noticeable that belonging to a Common Market had boosted considerably the economic development of the Six, while the UK, despite its EFTA membership, slipped behind. It was clear that the political and economic objectives enshrined in the Treaty of Rome had a dynamism not shared by the looser free-trade approach of the EFTA nations. A number of countries sought associated status with the EEC and Britain began to realise that it had to negotiate for entry.

Twice during the 1960s the UK applied for entry into the Community but was vetoed by the French President, General de Gaulle. By 1972, however, negotiations were successfully concluded and the UK – with Denmark and the Republic of Ireland – signed the Treaty of Rome and joined the Common Market on 1 January 1973.

The Labour government which came to power in 1974 decided that so momentous a decision, with important constitutional implications, should be put to a referendum of the British people. In 1975, after a major campaign with important figures from the main parties dividing into both camps, the 'Yes' to staying in campaign won by 67.2% to 32.8% of the vote. The UK electorate had voted two to one in favour of European integration.

First Greece, in 1981, and then, Spain and Portugal, in 1986, emerging as democracies after periods under right wing dictatorships, were welcomed into the EEC. In 1995, they were joined by Austria, Finland and Sweden.

Finding ways of encouraging a Community of twelve nations, and nine official languages, to work in harmony posed many problems, which were exacerbated by the first oil crisis of 1973 and another later in the decade with their severe effect upon production, employment and inflation. There were also problems with the protectionist policies of the Common Agricultural Policy which led to massive overproduction. The unwanted surpluses lasted until the Brussels summit of 1988, when British pressure forced their reduction using a system of stabilisers which brought the price down once a certain level of either production or market price was reached.

The coming of the internal market

From the 1970s onwards, the EC faced economic problems as it fell behind its main trading rivals: the US and Japan. Europe did not seem to be able to compete successfully with Japan and the newly emerging nations of the Pacific Rim – Hong Kong, South Korea, Taiwan and Singapore – most particularly in respect of high technology manufacturing.

This failure to compete was swiftly and dangerously translated in the 1970s and early 1980s into rising European unemployment figures which were dramatically worse than those of the US and Japan.

The Community related the reason for this failure to what became known as the 'Cost of non-Europe': an idea most clearly set out in a document known as the Cecchini Report. In the mid-1980s, Paolo Cecchini, an Italian economist working for the European Commission, made a number of studies, including a survey of over 11,000 business people throughout Europe, to seek their views about the cost to business of the remaining barriers to completely free trade in the European Community.

The results were startling: the cost of the physical barriers, such as waiting to get through customs and immigration and filling in forms, which were nominated by most business people as the most frustrating of all the barriers, was around twelve billion ECU. Discrimination against international tendering for public procurement contracts, accounting for over 15% of the European Community's GDP, cost the Community over 40 billion ECU or £28 billion. Most national and local governments discriminated in favour of home industries which stopped them buying the cheapest or most efficient goods or services.

The cost to industry of having different standards and specifications for different countries, almost impossible to quantify, was nevertheless probably the largest cost of all. For example, while a computer manufacturer in California could make one product available to all the other 49 states in the US and could, therefore, aim at a market of 240 million people, in Europe, each member state had its own specifications which required expensive modifications if goods were to be marketed throughout the EC. There could be no serious economy of scale, despite a potential market of 350 million, so long as such differences were maintained.

Finally, research and development costs were much increased by the fact that scientists and researchers had to work on different national projects rather than on wider European ones.

Cecchini also calculated that if these barriers were removed and if there could be a concerted macro-economic policy between the EC members, there would be a boost to job creation – a prediction difficult to quantify in the short term owing to the European recession of the late 1980s and early 1990s.

In order to remove these barriers and create a single European market, the European Community first needed enabling legislation. In 1986, an amendment to the Treaty of Rome was negotiated and was ratified by the parliaments of all twelve member states. Called the Single European Act (SEA), it combined a number of issues within its terms of reference:

- changes in the voting powers of the institutions,
- removal of barriers to trade,
- ensuring that a concern for the environment should be considered in all relevant EC legislation,
- economic and social cohesion (the transfer of funds from richer to poorer regions of the European Community),
- the social dimension (the protection of workers' rights and welfare),
- progress towards monetary union,
- progress towards political co-operation on foreign affairs.

The Act also introduced the Parliament's right to amend proposed legislation subject to qualified majority voting in the Council of Ministers. This applied to almost all legislation relating to the Single Market programme – an important step towards speeding up the legislative process. And, to set a tight timetable, the date for completion was set as the end of 1992.

Three Hundred Directives

A British Commissioner, Lord Cockfield, was put in charge of drafting the directives necessary to remove trade barriers and he outlined approximately three hundred proposals.

The legislative burden would have been greater if the Community had not moved from a policy of detailed harmonisation of standards to one of minimal harmonisation together with 'mutual recognition' i.e. if a product could legally be sold in one country, it should be accepted by the other member states. Areas that required harmonisation included

- health, including food, pharmaceuticals
- safety, including toys, building materials
- consumer protection in fields such as financial services, banks, insurance policies, mortgages
- academic, professional and vocational qualifications
- opening public procurement to Community-wide tender
- environmental standards

For the sake of procedural clarity, these directives were broken down into three groups:

- physical: customs and immigration (their agreement subject to unanimity in the Council)
- technical: mutual standards and specifications (decided by committees of the relevant trade representatives e.g. *Comité de Normalisation Européen* – CEN and CENELEC)
- fiscal: VAT and excise duties (also subject to unanimity).

In the event, there was no final agreement on VAT and excise controls and transitional measures are still in force. The removal of all controls on the free movement of people, in other words customs and immigration controls at internal borders, still await agreements over external European Union border controls and rights of asylum. Of course, even if agreements are reached on these issues, some countries, including the UK, may still refuse to remove their border controls even for European union citizens.

Eight member states – Germany, France, Italy, Belgium, the Netherlands, Luxembourg, Spain and Portugal – have pressed ahead with the removal of frontier controls between themselves by signing a special agreement known as the Schengen Agreement. Although it commits its signatories to remove their internal frontier controls, growing French hesitancy about its implications has delayed its full implementation.

Of course, the effectiveness of the single market depends a great deal on the willingness and ability of the member states to enforce the necessary legislation. This has varied considerably from one part of Europe to another and it would be naive to assume that in some parts outside tenders would stand much chance against local interests. Nevertheless, both the Commission and the European Court have attempted to enforce compliance.

5. Maastricht: a watershed?

The Single European Act (SEA) came about as an attempt to simplify the regulation of European markets and fulfil the original intention of the European Economic Community to create a genuine single market in which there would be complete freedom of movement for people, goods, capital and services. It also opened up new issues that would shortly require another IGC and a further treaty.

It was argued that the full potential of the single market would require the creation of a single currency. This had always been envisaged by the early founders of the EEC. No-one, however, foresaw the momentous and historic events that unfolded in 1989 as the fall of the Berlin wall signalled the end of the Communist era in Europe and the re-emergence of many historic and some new nations. New pressures were placed upon the process of European integration.

The early success of the EEC had been due, in part, to the desire for reconstruction and reconciliation. It was accelerated by the generous support it received from the USA through the Marshall Plan, which in turn owed much to American concerns that parts of Western Europe might, through choice or design, succumb to the expansion of the Communist Empire. In the event, the coming of the Iron Curtain served to reinforce the process of European integration and helped to cement the Atlantic Alliance.

The 'velvet' revolutions of 1989 have naturally had a considerable impact on the stability of the continent and also on the process of European integration. They removed an important stimulus for unity among the existing members of the EU, yet it soon became clear that newly emerging democracies wanted, and felt that they had a right to expect, early accession to the Union.

The other immediate consequence of the collapse of Communism was the opportunity for the re-unification of Germany which was seized by Chancellor Kohl with alacrity and determination. For the rest of Europe, however, the swift progress of German unification, which involved a very generous exchange rate for the East German currency, was not only to have a profound deflationary effect at a time when the world economy was already moving into a lengthy period of recession, but also to raise profound political anxieties.

Not all of this was apparent, however, to the leaders of the twelve member states of the European Union when they began the process of negotiations that led to the Treaty on European Union, frequently called the Maastricht Treaty. With hindsight it is possible to see that the favourable tide of public support that had carried through the Single European Act was beginning to turn and that it would be followed by a trough of uncertainty and scepticism. At the time, however, there was still sufficient optimism felt by those in power to believe that the momentum could be maintained towards the re-alisation of the next goal – that of economic and monetary union. It was a goal that was certainly not shared by all the participants, most particularly the British Government. In the event, referenda in Denmark and France revealed an unforeseen and remarkably high degree of scepticism towards the Treaty.

The style of the document that finally emerged from the negotia-tions on the morning of 11 December 1991 exacerbated public dis-content and confusion. It was a most inelegant and muddled piece of international legislation and its sheer incomprehensibility for most non-specialists meant that putting it before the general public served to increase its unpopularity.

The Maastricht Treaty was the culmination of long and arduous negotiations that had followed the reports of two IGCs between the twelve member states – one on Economic and Monetary Union and the other on Political Union. Its aim was to deal with the new op-portunities and problems resulting from the Single European Act by amending the Act and the previous treaties that had created the European Economic Community. Although its clumsy design led some observers to liken it to a camel, famously described as a horse designed by a committee, it was eventually approved by all the mem-ber states' parliaments, and in some countries by popular referenda.

The Maastricht Treaty contained five important ideas that made it different in kind from the previous treaties.

Firstly, it took the process of integration between the twelve member states a stage further and created new structures governing the relationship between both the member states and the institutions. In recognition of this development, and because the institutions of the existing European Economic Community were to form only one part of the new structure, the twelve member states agreed to form themselves into a 'European Union'.

While the Treaty developed and deepened the work of the Community as a whole, it also created two more areas of activity and decision-making, which would be largely conducted on an inter-governmental basis. This balanced the desire for further integration with a reluctance to give more power to the Community's institutions as a whole.

Whereas previously, most decisions were made through the institutions of the European Community (EC), the new European Union (EU) created by the Maastricht Treaty established a three-pillared structure, of which the European Community was just one, albeit the most important, pillar.

The three pillars of the European Union looked like this:

1. The European Community with, as before, the Council of Ministers, the European Parliament, the Commission and the Court of Justice;

2. Common Foreign and Security Policy (CSFP), to be agreed on an inter-governmental basis with some input from the other EC institutions; and

3. Justice and Home Affairs Policy, also to be agreed on an inter-governmental basis.

First it was simply the Common Market; then it became the European Economic Community; sometimes it was called the Community, bringing together the Coal and Steel Community, EURATOM and the EEC. As the European Economic Community had to deal with an increasing number of political, environmental and social issues, it became logical to drop the qualifying word 'economic'. From now on, the EC will be used to mean those institutions that the European Union has in common, excluding the two separate pillars.

The Maastricht Treaty delineates the Community's main tasks and together they reveal the scope of the activities which today fall broadly under the heading of 'European'.

- forming a common market
- creating economic and monetary union
- maintaining sustainable and non-inflationary growth
- respecting the environment
- maintaining a high level of employment and social protection
- raising living standards in member states
- encouraging economic and social cohesion.

These are the goals and the key competences allocated to the European level of government. In addition, the Treaty also listed the following aims:

- eliminating all customs duties and restrictions on importing and exporting goods within the Union
- introducing measures for a common immigration and visa policy into the Union
- providing for a common commercial policy (for example when negotiating external treaties like the General Agreement on Tariffs and Trade (GATT)
- removing any remaining obstacles to the free movement of people, goods, capital and services within the Union
- promoting measures concerning the entry and movement of people in the internal market
- developing common policies in agriculture and fisheries
- pursuing a common policy in transport
- ensuring that competition is not distorted in the internal market

- approximating the laws of member states to the extent required for the functioning of a common market
- promoting research and technological development
- encouraging the establishment and development of trans-European transport networks
- contributing to the attainment of a high level of health protection
- contributing to the quality education and training and to the flowering of the cultures of member states
- co-ordinating policy in the sphere of overseas development co-operation
- contributing to the strengthening of consumer protection, and
- promoting measures in the spheres of energy, civil protection and tourism.

These are not areas in which the Community has exclusive authority but rather areas of co-operation between the European, national and, at times, regional and local levels of government. But they are issues which, at the European level, concern the institutions of the European Community – the Council, the Parliament, the Commission and the Court.

Secondly, the Treaty established a principle in the European Union which reinforced the concept of 'subsidiarity'. Subsidiarity refers to whether decisions should be taken at a European institutional level or by the relevant institutions in the member states, which legislation should be adopted by the governments of the member states, and who should be responsible for its enforcement.

The relevant clause in the Treaty states that in the areas which do not fall under its executive jurisdiction, the Community will only take action when the objectives cannot be sufficiently achieved by the member states.

The Community is legally bound to adhere to this principle and no doubt it will be the subject of litigation before the Court of Justice. Quite clearly, some policies can only be achieved through collective Community action. For example, removing the barriers to create an open market can only be achieved if each country accepts the rules and plays by them. This means the Community has to insist on certain standards which, for some people whose interests may be harmed by them, has seemed both irritating and unnecessary.

It does not take a great deal of thought to realise that a product should be safe if it is to be sold across borders. The failure to ensure common standards would swiftly lead to chaos and confusion not to mention genuine health and safety problems. For example, the failure to ensure safe pharmaceuticals, foodstuffs and building materials could lead to loss of life. Similarly, everyone from pensioners to investment companies needs to be certain that common and sufficiently high financial regulations apply throughout the Community if they are to avoid being swindled.

On the other hand, it is increasingly important to many people that the Community does not meddle in areas that can best be handled by national, regional or even local governments.

The principle of subsidiarity was designed to prevent a widespread, though not always accurate, feeling that citizens in the member states are having decisions made for them in Brussels that they would prefer to have taken either by their national, regional or local governments.

Thirdly, a new Committee of the Regions with the limited right to offer its advice and suggestions, was set up in response to a growing feeling, in many member states, that the regions and local authorities of Europe should have a greater say in the Community's future.

Fourthly, the Treaty set out a procedure and timetable for creating economic and monetary union, a process under which the existing currencies of the twelve member states would be replaced by a single currency controlled by a European Central Bank. The timetable suggested made it possible for a single currency to be introduced in some member states as early as 1997, though more probably in 1999. Only those countries whose economies have converged in accordance with criteria laid down by the Treaty will be able to adopt the single currency. The European Central Bank is to be an independent institution, free of political control, though answerable for its management to the Union's other institutions. The British Government, however, unwilling to commit itself at that stage to the principle of a single currency, was allowed an opt-out clause in the Treaty.

Fifthly, the Treaty raised for the first time the issue of European citizenship. This gave new, albeit limited, shared rights to all those presently citizens of the member states. Among these are:

- the right to move freely from country to country within the Union, subject to the country's laws (such as, in some cases, requiring proof that a person will not require social assistance and has adequate health insurance)
- the right to vote and stand as a candidate in local and European parliamentary elections in whichever member state a citizen resides i.e. the right to vote in these elections will be based upon residency, not nationality, though this will not apply to national general elections
- the right to diplomatic or consular representation by the diplomatic or consular authorities of any member state if you get into trouble in a third country (i.e. one that is not a member state of the EU)
- the right to bring complaints about maladministration by Community institutions before an Ombudsman appointed by the European Parliament and able to conduct independent investigations into allegations.

European citizenship does not in any way remove, reduce or conflict with the rights and responsibilities of national citizenship but rather adds a new dimension to the lives of those who belong to the Union's member states.

Further to these five central ideas, the Treaty also set out to reform or enhance other Community structures and activities but these, while important, were not new in kind.

The Treaty gave limited extended powers to the EP. Although they did not go as far towards remedying the 'democratic deficit' – the lack of democracy in the Community's decision-making procedures – as many reformers wished, the Parliament received greater powers to amend legislation and, in some cases, to veto it if joint negotiations with the Council of Ministers failed to reach an agreed text for new laws.

The Treaty also increased the Community's powers to enforce certain social rights and obligations but, because of the British government's refusal to accept this part of the Treaty, known as the Social Chapter, it was put into a separate protocol signed by the other eleven members states.

Various steps were also agreed to tighten up the Community's finances:

- when proposing new spending measures, the Commission must now give assurances that it can be financed within the limits of existing European Community financial resources

- the status of the European Court of Auditors, who check everything is in correct financial order, was enhanced, making it a full EC institution

- the European Parliament was given the right to ask the Commission to give evidence regarding spending and financial control. The Commission then has to act on the decisions and observations of the Parliament

- Governments were obliged to treat fraud affecting the Community's financial interests in the same way that they dealt with fraud affecting national finances

- Finally, the Court of Justice was given greater powers to ensure that all member states meet their obligations to enforce Community legislation. Those who do not could in future be fined by the Court.

This, then, is the situation that confronts the forthcoming IGC. From the original proposals to bring continental coal and steel production under common ownership there has developed an institutional framework to both govern and facilitate the complex inter-relationships between a steadily increasing number of member states. The European Union was not constructed according to a blue-print but developed *sui generis*. Much of its strength and dynamism can be traced to Monnet's belief in creating common institutions to meet day to day the needs of the member states rather than attempting to fit events into some theoretical construction. But maybe the time has arrived when the benefits of organic growth need to be complemented by the discipline of bringing greater coherence and definition to the whole project. Does Europe really need a new constitution, pulling all these disparate parts into a single, simpler framework?

6. The ghosts in the machine: procedures, institutions, committees

Considering the number of areas and issues covered by the European Union, it is perhaps surprising that the Community's institutions are as little known as they are. Much confusion arises from the lack of clarity (most noticeably in the tabloid press and some other popular parts of the media) about the institutions and how they work.

The Commission

Twenty Commissioners are appointed by the governments of the member states for fixed terms of five years. They head a team of some 25,000 European civil servants, sometimes known as Euro-crats, who work in twenty-two General Directorates, the equivalent at European level of national ministries. Two Commissioners are appointed from the larger countries and one each from the smaller countries. The current President of the Commission is Jacques Santer, a Luxembourger, appointed by the governments of the member states for five years from January 1995.

The Commission's job is:

- to initiate legislation necessary to fulfil the aims and objectives of the treaties
- to carry out legislation approved by the Parliament and the Council of Ministers
- to ensure the application of the treaties and Community legislation and to ensure compliance.

In other words, it is the Commission's duty to propose legislation that will benefit Europe as a whole and then to make sure it is carried out by the member states.

It is neither through accident nor overweening ambition that the Commission has a virtual monopoly over the initiation of legislation. It was seen, from the very beginning, as the way to ensure that European integration could be driven forward and would not become bogged down by the competing political and economic interests of the member states.

The Commission's role is clearly circumscribed, but it exercises considerable power and authority. The sole right to propose legislation is of vital importance in determining both the direction and the speed in which the Union as a whole will travel. Thus, the Commission has become the focus for all pressure groups, including national governments, who wish to see the introduction or amendment of legislation within the European Community's competence. The Commission is also responsible for the administration of a large part of the European Community's budget.

Unfortunately, the tendency of many critics of the European Union as a whole to level their attacks at the Commission has obscured real failings that require reform. The problem is not that the Commission is overstaffed – it is smaller than many local authorities – nor that it is unapproachable or secretive – it is surprisingly open at all levels and willing to listen to a multitude of opinions and interests. Its main weaknesses appear to be its attachment to harmonisation in areas that might be best left to individual choice and, ironically for those who argue for greater inter-governmentalism, that it is still too linked to the national governments because of the need to maintain national staff quotas.

Despite a considerable shift of emphasis from harmonisation to the principle of mutual recognition under which the rules and regulations applicable to goods and services in operation in one member state are deemed to be appropriate throughout the Union unless challenged on grounds of health, safety or consumer protection, the Commission still seems unduly fond of trying to define and regulate wide areas of commercial activity. Although it is usually acting from the best motives – to protect citizens from the dangers implicit in unrestricted trade – there are times when the citizens may prefer to take their own risks.

While it is hard to deny that food, for example, should be as fresh and hygienically prepared as possible, there should still be room for those who might prefer to risk the slight dangers to health involved in the consumption of, say, products made with unpasteurised milk, in the hope of a rewarding flavour or texture. The danger is not that the Commission may impose bad laws but rather that it has a tendency to try and restrict a natural human desire to exercise freedom even if, at times, it may involve a degree of irresponsiblity.

There is also the danger that, as long as national quotas restrict the ability to appoint the Commission strictly on merit, strict impartiality in decision-making will be compromised by national interest. There will also be a resistance to the need for a complete overhaul of procedures and working methods that could greatly improve the insititution's efficiency.

What is required is a reform of the structure and practices of the Commission as an institution within the context of its existing role in the framework of the Union as a whole.

The European Parliament

The EP is directly elected by the people of Europe every five years. Its 626 members, MEPs, sit in party groups, such as Socialists (including the British Labour Party), the European People's Party (including the German Christian Democrats and the British Conservatives), the European Liberal, Democrat and Reform Group, Greens, Communists and assorted small parties, including the Far Right, who sit with a handful of independents. Although they sit in party groups, European parliamentarians represent and frequently fight hard to protect and promote the interests of their countries and constituents – but they do so under the umbrella of the pan-European political groupings to which they belong.

The idea that certain key political objectives can only be achieved through concerted multi-national activity is central to the views of many who subscribe to a belief in an integrated Europe. Many of the central political and economic issues of our times are no longer confined within national borders. The very idea of building socialism or a free market system within the borders of any one country alone is patently absurd. Political and economic interdependence is growing throughout the world and within Europe in particular. Nevertheless, substantial ideological differences remain between, for example, those who wish to see the role of government reduced and those who believe in its power to change society. Similar divisions still exist on a whole range of political and social issues that are simplistically pigeon-holed as 'left' and 'right'. The EP offers a forum for legislation to be debated within the context of these ideological divides, in contrast to the Council of Ministers for whom national interest, as defined by the majority view in home parliaments, is the determining factor.

One of the great strengths of the European system is that legislation is subject to both pressures. For it to be fully realised, however, requires a real balance in the power and authority of the two institutions.

The EP originally had only an advisory and supervisory role, but its powers were extended considerably by the Single European Act and the Maastricht Treaty. It now has the right to pass or withhold the budget, to approve or sack the Commission, to amend legislation and, in certain major areas, including the internal market, consumer protection, health, education and general environmental programmes, the Parliament has joint decision-making powers with the Council of Ministers.

Essentially, the EP can affect legislation under four different procedures. It can simply be consulted on certain matters, for example the nomination of members of the Executive Board of the future European Bank, but its opinion has no binding force. Secondly, it may take part in the co-operation procedure under which it may propose amendments to proposed legislation that can only be rejected by the Council acting unanimously (the co-operation procedure applies to most aspects of single market legislation). Thirdly, in certain areas, notably with reference to some aspects of economic and monetary union and for treaties with third countries, Parliament's assent is required for legislation to be adopted. And finally, under the Maastricht Treaty, it was given certain powers of co-decision on certain aspects of legislation with the Council of Ministers. If agreement cannot be reached with the Council in a joint Conciliation Committee, the Parliament can reject a proposal by an overall majority of its members.

In addition, if the EP agrees by an overall majority that new European legislation is necessary, it can request the Commission to submit proposals. It can also, at the request of a quarter of its members, set up a temporary Committee of Inquiry to investigate serious issues such as fraud. And it has appointed an Ombudsman to investigate contravention or maladministration in the implementation of Community law, a crucial new benefit for all European citizens who can turn to him to investigate areas where they believe the Community's institutions to have acted wrongly. Citizens may turn to Parliament's Petition Committee for problems relating to national and local abuses of power.

The Parliament meets in Strasbourg and Brussels and also has offices in Luxembourg. This is a cumbersome situation that wastes close to £100 million per year in unnecessary travel and lost time. The situation will only change when the Heads of Government have the courage to upset either the French, the Belgian or the Luxembourg authorities.

The Council of Ministers

There is not one Council of Ministers but several: Environment, Trade, Finance, Education, Health etc., each bringing together ministers from relevant departments. Twice a year, at European Council meetings, the Heads of State and Government meet to make overall decisions for the whole Union and every month the Foreign Ministers meet to try to co-ordinate everything that is going on. The Council of Ministers is backed up by a permanent staff based in Brussels and by home civil servants travelling to meet in Brussels with them.

Nor does the Council of Ministers always meet in Brussels. For three months every year – April, June and October – they and their staff travel instead to Luxembourg, incurring additional expense and taking extra time. The Council of Ministers and the European Council usually take decisions by consensus, that is to say by unanimity, with any state having a veto if it feels its vital interests are at stake. However, since 1987 when the SEA came into effect considerably more decisions are taken by a system known as qualified majority voting (QMV). This gives Germany, France, the UK and Italy 10 votes each, Spain 8 votes, Belgium, Greece, the Netherlands and Portugal 5 votes each, Austria and Sweden 4 votes, Denmark, Ireland and Finland 3 votes and Luxembourg 2 votes. For a proposal to be accepted, it requires 62 votes out of the available 87. The system is designed to prevent the large countries alone outvoting the small ones and vice-versa.

Three times a year, the Heads of State and Government of the member states meet together with the President of the European Commission in order to discuss the key issues facing the European Union and to make strategic decisions. Each member state takes the Presidency of the Union for six months in an alphabetical rotation and the country holding the Presidency is responsible for setting the agenda, chairing all the Council meetings, and for representing the Union in external matters during that time.

Does this sound complicated? It is. This is why changes to these procedures are being considered by the next IGC with a view to reducing and simplifying the many ways in which legislation passes through the institutions.

The European Court of Justice

The European Court of Justice (ECJ) interprets Community legislation and resolves disputes. It is based in Luxembourg and should not be confused with the Court of Human Rights which sits in Strasbourg.

The Court is composed of fifteen Judges appointed from the member states and 9 Advocates General whose job it is to represent the facts of the case to the Court in a reasoned submission.

Essentially the Court judges the 'legality' of Community legislation. Actions may be brought before it by one of the institutions, by a member state or by legal organisations, including businesses or individuals, directly affected by a particular regulation or decision. For example, the Commission may take a member state before the Court if it believes that insufficient action has been taken to enforce a certain area of Community law.

With over 400 cases being referred to the European Court annually, it takes an average of two years for actions to be finally resolved. Should the ECJ also be required in the future to interpret the European Convention on Human Rights and Personal Freedoms, presently under the sole authority of the European Court of Human Rights in Strasbourg, its case load would increase considerably.

It is the Court which, more than any other institution, has defined the degree to which the European Union has already developed a quasi-federal status. Not only does it represent the rule of law which must underlie any serious attempt to control the persistent recourse of nation states to violence in order to extend or protect national interests, but its judgements have illustrated a belief that the legal status of the European Union as a whole is greater than the sum of its parts. Its responsibility to define subsidiarity and other constitutional issues has developed its role as a kind of Constitutional Supreme Court for Europe.

In its first opinion on the European Economic Area, which preceded the accession of some members of the EFTA into the European Union, the ECJ confirmed that:

> The EEC Treaty, albeit concluded in the form of an international agreement, nonetheless constitutes the constitutional charter of a Community based on the rule of law ... The essential characteristics of the Community legal order which has thus been established are in particular its primacy over the law of the member states and the direct effect of a whole series of provisions which are applicable to their nationals and to the member states themselves.

The Court has recognised the 'constitutional' nature of the Treaties, the gradual transition over 40 years from customs union, to common market, economic and monetary union and a form of political union. This does not mean, however, that the ECJ is the European Supreme Court. Far from it: such a role would give it inordinate and unsupported authority in areas of national legislation. But it does mean that, in some areas, most especially in the Court's acceptance of multi-national legislation in certain areas and in the Commission's ability to conduct certain international negotiations, for example during the GATT talks, on behalf of the member states, the European Union has some of the 'personality' attributed to a federal state.

This should come as no surprise to any legislator or informed spectator. Back in 1974, Lord Denning prophesied that: "The Treaty is like an incoming tide. It flows into the estuaries and up the rivers. It cannot be held back." Community law is and will remain superior to English and Scottish law and must therefore take precedence over UK Acts of Parliament; it is also clear that the European Court is right to 'freeze' national law until its compatibility with EC law is tested. As T.C Hartley emphasises in *The Foundations of European Community Law*:

> It is a basic rule of Community law that a directly effective provision of Community law always prevails over a provision of national law. This rule, which is not found in any of the Treaties but has been proclaimed with great emphasis by the Court, applies irrespective of the nature of the Community provision (Constitutive Treaty, Community act or agreement with a non-member state) or that of the national provision (constitution, statute or subordinate legislation); it also applies irrespective of whether the Community provision came before, or after, the national provision: in all cases the national provision must give way to Community law.

Whether this is a satisfactory state of affairs is open to debate. The German Constitutional Court questioned it prior to Germany's agreeing the Maastricht Treaty, and the Danish Court of Appeal has entered a *caveat* more recently regarding the abrogation of aspects of national sovereignty to the Union. But it shows the degree to which the European Union has moved in the full knowledge of its legislators, including the British Parliament, towards a federal system.

Other European Community Institutions

Just to complete the picture, I should add a brief word about a cluster of European bodies set up by the treaties which have a role to play in building Europe. They include:

- The European Investment Bank (EIB) which provides extremely large sums to finance capital investment in the member states. Its report each year lists the major public and private projects that have been assisted by EIB loans.

- The Economic and Social Committee (ECOSOC), which brings together representatives from all sectors of working life, including employers and producers organisations, farmers, unions, crafts-people, and the professions in order to advise the Council of Ministers on certain legislation. With 222 members, appointed by the member states, ECOSOC acts as an expert consultative committee and sounding-board on a broad range of public and specialised issues.

- The Committee of the Regions. Set up under the Maastricht Treaty as a response to the growing awareness of the importance of regional identity and local government, the Committee of the Regions has 222 members appointed or elected from regional and local authorities who must be consulted by the Commission and the Council on all relevant matters.

- The Court of Auditors, as its name implies, monitors and audits all aspects of the income and expenditure of the Union and seeks to uncover fraud. Bearing in mind that most fraud remains the responsibility of the member states, it has been proposed that the duty of the member states' internal auditors and national audit boards to co-operate with Court of Auditors to combat fraud should be made more explicit.

7. The calm before the storm: the Reflection Group

European integration has tended to follow a pattern of great leaps forward followed by periods of consolidation. Both economic and monetary union and the enlargement of the Union to the east are destined to be great leaps but a certain hesitation on the part of some member states is causing a degree of unease and uncertainty before they leap. As with all bold adventures, however, success depends to a very great extent upon confidence. Like fifteenth-century sailors, whose journeys to the new world were as much an act of faith and determination as of knowledge or science, so the next major steps in the evolution of European unity depend as much upon political will as upon economic necessity. Nor are the institutions that will have to undertake this voyage the most sleek and elegant of vessels. In fact, the IGC must try and make them seaworthy. Hopefully, it will employ better craftsmen than those who constructed the Maastricht Treaty.

Detailed preparation was required before discussions could begin. To help give a structure to the IGC, a think-tank known as the Reflection Group was created, comprising one nominee from each member state alongside representatives of the Commission and the EP. The Group's tasks were to represent the views of the member states and the institutions, to receive suggestions from interested and relevant groups and to prepare an agenda for the conference itself. While it had the task of presenting and coordinating the many and various opinions, it was not given the right to negotiate any agreement. That was left to the IGC itself.

The European Council, comprising the Heads of State and Government, wanted to avoid re-opening the Maastricht discussions, since they had given rise to extremely divisive debates in several countries. This IGC was simply to be a revision of minor aspects of that treaty that needed updating. But the limited brief given to the Reflection Group actually raised a large number of important questions.

The three main areas entrusted to the group for examination and which now confront the IGC itself are:

- how to make Europe more relevant to its citizens,
- how to enable the Union to work better and preparing it for enlargement, and
- giving the Union greater capacity for external action.

As was evident in the Group's report and in the flurry of newspaper articles that greeted the start of the IGC, these rather innocuous sounding headings in fact open up most of the important points of debate I listed in chapter 3. In one way or another, they affect all of them directly except the budget, which is not due for review until the end of the century, and the commitment to economic and monetary union, which none of the participants wants to reopen at the moment.

Even so, the proximity of economic and monetary union will have an enormous bearing upon the IGC's conclusions and vice versa. It is almost impossible to reach conclusions about the political structures of the European Union without taking into account the political implications of economic and monetary union. Whether or not it is correct to assert that economic and monetary union would lead inexorably to political union, it is certainly disingenuous to suggest that the former would not impact powerfully upon the latter.

Economic and monetary union will of necessity require close coordination of macro-economic policy and some areas of fiscal policy between participating member states. The political question, like so many others in the European debate, is which decisions should be made by a Central Bank, which by inter-governmental agreement and how far democratically elected bodies, at the European or national parliamentary level will or should be involved.

Thus while it will not be discussed, the implications of economic and monetary union in the future will have a powerful influence upon the IGC's deliberations.

Meanwhile, in offices and meeting rooms throughout the fifteen member states, committees representing every conceivable European interest group and political party busied themselves in submitting to the Reflection Group their own suggestions and recommendations for inclusion on the IGC agenda. Most of the papers and documents submitted concentrate on key areas of reform, particularly changes in the working procedures of the main institutions, the possibility of integrating the work of the two inter-governmental pillars – CFSP and Justice and Home Affairs – of the European Union into the Community structures and the need to increase accountability, democracy, transparency and subsidiarity in the working of the Union as a whole.

In fact, it is interesting how closely, with relatively few exceptions, most groups who submitted ideas shared a common purpose. From political parties, interest groups, and indeed from the institutions themselves the emphasis was primarily on institutional reform, particularly the need to increase the Union's openness and accountability. Most groups addressed the distribution of powers and competences between the institutions of the Union and the balance of power between European institutions on the one hand and the member states on the other, including considerable pressure to integrate the two inter-governmental pillars – Justice and Home Affairs and Foreign and Security Policy into the central pillar of the European Community's institutions. Not surprisingly, the solutions proffered varied as much as the bodies that submitted them, but they illustrated well the main problems that needed addressing.

Widening or deepening

One of the underlying themes of European integration has been how to maintain a balance between strengthening relations between existing members states and enlarging the group by accepting new members who inevitably put new pressures on existing institutions and structures. This debate between 'widening and deepening' is resolved each time in practice by conceding a little of each. But soon we shall be faced with a situation altogether different in scale. Having increased its membership from six to fifteen over the last forty years, the European Union is confronted with the prospect of doubling again within another decade. And there is a growing impatience among the newly democratic nations of Central and Eastern Europe to have their applications for admission processed speedily.

But it is clear that the IGC will have to supply answers to a number of pertinent questions before it will be practicable to widen the European borders in the way that the supporters of further enlargement are urging.

There is already unease in some member states who feel the pace of integration is too quick. Can institutions designed for six really meet the needs of fifteen, 25 or 30 members, or will they have to be radically revised? Can the institutions, as they are now, cope with the implications of another 130 million people? The EU would then encompass close to 500 million people. How large should the EP become? If every member state demands a Commissioner of its own, full translation and interpretation facilities in its own language and the right to hold the Presidency of the European Union every six months, will the whole operation become unmanageable?

And what about the cost? Richer countries have, up till now, been prepared to contribute to the development of the poorer regions of Europe in exchange for access to wider markets – but will they be prepared to foot the vastly increased bill if the European Union expands to include the developing economies of Central and Eastern Europe which will need considerable support for several years more?

For example, the cost of integrating the four most likely early entrants – Poland, Hungary, the Czech Republic and Slovenia – might mean an increase of 75 per cent in the EU budget if they join at the turn of the century. The financial cost of further enlargement may look high especially at a time when every domestic pressure is towards tax reduction. On the other hand, the implications for security in Europe if the Iron Curtain were to be perversely rebuilt by the west on economic grounds would certainly prove even more costly.

If widening is to be a priority, however, what will it mean for the existing member states' chances of properly establishing the single market and adopting a single currency? If enlargement takes place first, will it prevent the introduction of a single currency because of the very wide disparity between individual economies? Or, bearing in mind that not all existing member states may necessarily move forward towards a single currency together, could new entrants be offered the opportunity to join the monetary union at a later date? Would it encourage an approach to membership known as 'variable geometry' where all members aim for the same goals but choose separate timescales within which to reach them, some sooner, some later?

Should all member states move forward to a defined and agreed goal simultaneously or can an argument be made for a multi-speed or 'variable geometry' process of integration? So far, with the exception of a few individually negotiated 'opt-outs', the member states of the European Union have all moved forward together, treaty by treaty. But in this IGC some may argue that each could go forward at its own speed. Is this acceptable, or should progress be confined to the pace of the slowest?

In an attempt to find solutions to some of these problems and to deal with the wish of some current member states to opt-out of some sections of the existing treaties, (for example the UK's opt-out of the monetary union and social provisions in the Maastricht Treaty) a number of ideas of varying complexity have been put forward.

One suggestion for enabling the more committed member states to move forward at a faster pace was contained in a paper put forward by two senior members of the ruling German Christian Democratic Party, Wolfgang Schäuble and Karl Lamers, in 1994. They suggested that a hard core of countries might wish to press ahead with a common currency and closer foreign and security decision-making procedures, rather than wait for all the members of the EU to be in agreement. They specifically did not rule out the others catching up, but neither did they want to be held back. At the heart of this inner core would be Germany, France and Benelux but a helping hand would be offered to those countries that had the political will to join, even if it might take time for their economies to meet the necessary criteria.

But, what if this inner group decided on other issues ahead of the meetings of the Council? Would it mean the development of an inner elite leadership that other member states would have to follow, a caucus inside the Council? Clearly if such an inner group were established, it might well reach agreement on a whole variety of issues, making it a powerful, possibly dominant lobby in any discussions between all the member states.

Although this idea, which would lead to a two-speed, or even a multi-speed Europe, has been dismissed for the time being, it is by no means impossible that it will be reintroduced later. Not surprisingly, it was opposed not only by those who wanted Europe to go more slowly, but also by many who did not approve of the idea of the member states being divided into faster and slower camps. The idea's supporters, however, argued that those countries that did not want to go faster should not hold up those that did: an argument worth remembering when looking at the question of whether individual member states should continue to hold a veto over legislation indefinitely.

Another suggestion developed from disagreements about the purpose of European integration. It became known as 'Europe *à la carte*', because it allowed for different member states to sign up to different areas of the Union's activities. Apart from the existing treaties and legislation, they could choose whether or not to go further on certain issues, for example economic and monetary union, CFSP or the social dimension. Effectively European integration on the present model would come to a halt, and a plethora of new, smaller groupings would press ahead in different areas of common interest, free from the institutional framework of the Commission, Parliament and Court of Justice.

To achieve a greater focus against such a complex background it was necessary for some guiding principles to be defined by the Reflection Group. A clear majority rejected the idea of multi-speed or '*à la carte*' Europe, but recognised that without a certain degree of flexibility the whole project could founder. They proposed, therefore, the following formula:

- flexibility should be allowed only when it works to the benefit of the Union's objectives as a whole, and if all other solutions have been ruled out, and then only on a case by case basis,

- that any differences in the degree of integration should only be temporary,
- that no one member state which succeeds in meeting all the previously agreed and necessary conditions should be excluded from participating fully in any given action or common policy,
- that provision should be made for measures to assist those who want to take part in a given action or policy but are temporarily unable to do so,
- that when allowing for flexibility, all existing European laws (the '*acquis communautaire*') must be maintained,
- that, as far as possible, decisions should be taken through the European Community's institutions rather than through separate inter-governmental structures,
- derogations (the process by which some countries are allowed not to comply with certain changes that may be particularly difficult) should not be allowed if they jeopardise the internal market and go against competition,

From this outline it is clear that the underlying strategy of the Reflection Group has been to urge a moderate degree of reform without undermining either the existing structures or the pattern of relations between the existing member states. Its final conclusions will be analysed in later chapters, but there is clearly a danger that it has fallen between two stools without fully satisfying the key protagonists at either extreme of the argument. An even greater danger is that the resulting negotiations in the IGC could fail to capture public imagination because they will not be radical enough.

There were dissenting views within the group, faithfully recorded as a minority opinion (frequently recognisable as the UK representative's opinions). For that minority even the smallest movement towards reform was too much and would be fiercely resisted. If this proves to be the case in the IGC itself and yet another fumbling compromise has to be found, the chances of it finding public support will be limited.

8. Keeping the house in order: reforming the institutions

At the top of the agenda of the IGC is the issue of institutional reform. What exactly does this mean?

Negotiators have two key questions to ask themselves: firstly, are these structures satisfactory in the sense that they serve the citizens of Europe adequately by being open, efficient, accountable and democratic? Secondly, can they meet the challenges that will derive from the further enlargement of the Community?

In the Reflection Group's terms of reference, these objectives were outlined in such a way as to define more precisely the tasks that need to be tackled and, at the same time, to open many issues up for wider discussion, specifically:

- analysing the principles and objectives of the Union, and the way it should implement its decisions,
- looking for ways to make the institutions more democratic and open so that they are able to adjust to the demands of an enlarged Union,
- strengthening public support for the process of European integration by meeting the need for a form of democracy which would be closer to the citizens of Europe,
- putting the principle of subsidiarity into practice more effectively.

All the while, the Reflection Group, and subsequently the IGC, had to remember the impact on the European Union's budget and the potential impact of economic and monetary union.

David Martin, one of the UK's Vice-Presidents and a respected MEP, once remarked that, if the European Union as a whole applied to join itself, its application would almost certainly be rejected because of a lack of internal democracy. This is a harsh but justified judgement on what has become known as the 'democratic deficit'. The problem was remedied to some extent by reforms contained in the Maastricht Treaty, which increased the legislative powers of the EP. Nevertheless, criticism is still justified and will remain so unless and until the IGC deals seriously with some of the major anomalies that exist in the decision-making processes of the European Union's institutions.

A related problem most people have is trying to understand how the European Union works. It could best be summarised by posing a question which many people would like answered in the simplest and clearest way: "What powers in Europe are exercised at what level and by whom, and to whom are the decision makers accountable?"

Encapsulated in this question are possibly the most fundamental issues the IGC will need to deal with if the EU is to be able to command popular support and loyalty. Essentially, the problem breaks down into the four following groups of questions: is the EU efficient? Is the EU accountable? Is the EU open? Is the EU democratic?

Efficient?

Does the European Commission have too much power in general, or, perhaps, not enough in some areas and too much in others? Do the European institutions work efficiently, or are they bureaucracies in need of reform? If and when the European Union enlarges to more than twenty members, can every country expect to have the same level of representation as at present, or will a new system need to be devised? Should qualified majority voting be extended for the sake of efficiency, or should the use of the veto be extended to protect national sovereignty? Should there be an alternative voting system that requires votes cast to represent a majority of the population as well as a majority of governments? And how should a proper balance between large and small countries be maintained as more states – most of them relatively small ones – join the Union?

Accountable?

Is the existing system properly accountable to the citizens of Europe, as represented in either the EP or national parliaments, or does it fall between the two stools? Indeed, is the Council of Ministers, which is free to conduct its meetings behind closed doors, properly accountable at all if there can be no public scrutiny of its meetings? Theoretically, ministers are accountable to their national parliaments, but a lack of information and the near impossibility of reversing decisions make that something of a hollow claim. Is the British Parliament able to influence sufficiently the workings of the European Union or even control its own government's activities within the Union?

Open?

Can ordinary European citizens really discover what is being done in their name at the European level or is there a failure to explain and publicise decisions taken? And when it is published, is legislation clear and coherent or couched in language understandable only to lawyers and Eurocrats? The Commission has certainly expended considerable effort and resources trying to publicise and explain the European Union's laws and policies but do you feel that somewhere along the line the message has not always got through to the person on the street? Could some governments be failing to play their part? Or is there a much deeper problem that will need to be resolved in the long term through educational initiatives in schools and colleges and, indeed, by providing more balanced information to the general public?

Democratic?

How real is the 'democratic deficit' and can it be substantially overcome within the present system? Is the EP already sufficiently involved in the decision-making process or should its role in the legislative process be extended? At the moment, the 'co-decision' process between the EP and the Council of Ministers, as outlined in a previous chapter, only applies to some areas of European legislation, for example the completion of the single market and some environmental issues. It does not apply, for example, to the CAP, to Foreign and Security Policy or Justice and Home Affairs, in the latter two areas because decisions are taken by unanimity between the member states. Should it apply to these policy issues as well?

Should the EP be more closely involved with the appointment of Commissioners or should this power remain primarily in the hands of the member states? Is the relationship between the EP and the national parliaments of the member states satisfactory or could it be improved? Indeed should national parliaments be more involved in European decision-making to the extent of forming a second chamber? Should the Commission be made to account for its actions more fully to the EP? Is it possible or desirable that one day the Commission might be elected by the EP or perhaps even by the people of Europe directly?

Is there an adequate balance between decisions made at the European level and those reserved to the nation state? Should there be a clearer definition of where power lies, or even a greater devolution of power not just to the national but perhaps the regional or local level of government? Or perhaps further areas of competence – for example, defence and security – should become the prerogative of the Union as a whole. Deciding which powers should be allocated at which level and by whom will surface time and again during the IGC because they are questions which go to the very heart of the European debate.

Clearly, such questions are not restricted to the IGC. They are being openly raised and discussed by many groups and individuals both sympathetic and hostile to the European Union. Among the most interesting has been Sir James Goldsmith's analysis of Europe's problems in his book *The Trap*. As a deeply considered and challenging series of extended reflections about many of the world's most pressing social, political and environmental problems, the book offers occasional original and important insights. The section dealing with Europe, however, seems confused and gives a strange misreading of the themes and objectives of European integration.

Sir James argues that "decentralisation must be the fundamental principle on which Europe is built". He also claims that the EP is a "pseudo-democratic institution" and that "the weaker the national institutions, the stronger are those in Brussels". In a sense, all three statements, depending upon how one defines the principles of subsidiarity and accountability, contain an element of truth. But they do not contain the whole truth. Federalism, of which the principle of subsidiarity is a central tenet, is concerned with the decentralisation of power. It is also true that, at the moment, in the UK, the struggle for power is between the national government and Brussels. But this is not the case everywhere, nor need it be. In Germany, the *Länder* guard their powers and competencies as fiercely as the Federal Government protects its own authority.

For as long as Sir James and others believe that most of the business currently undertaken by the EP should be the role of national parliaments, they are bound to see the EP as "pseudo-democratic" or, again in Sir James's words, "a waste of time or downright destructive". The EP is caught in a double bind: when it had few powers, it was considered ineffectual; when it attempts to exercise its authority, it is damned for interfering in the affairs of the member states and national parliaments.

But are national parliaments truly able to deal with European legislation? A problem arises because the Council's decisions are rarely, if ever, adequately scrutinised by national parliaments, even in Britain. As Anthony Bevin pointed out in *The Independent* on 20 August 1996: "MPs' attempts to apply the basic checks of British democracy to European law are being undermined by a staggering mix of Whitehall incompetence and Brussels arrogance." The Commons Select Committee on European Legislation revealed that only five out of 14 government departments even bothered to order relevant reports from HMSO; vital ministerial letters are routinely sent to wrong addresses or even non-existent committees; and, "over the past twelve months, 75 Brussels proposals of legal or political importance had to be examined 'blind' – with no official texts available from Brussels."

Technically, ministers are not allowed – except in the most exceptional circumstances – to agree to legislation in Brussels ministerial meetings, without prior passage through the Westminster scrutiny process. In fact, as the Committee reports, there have been a number of lapses of that rule, in breach of government pledges to Parliament, or even in defiance of Commons resolutions. Without the involvement of the EP, there would be little democratic control over the process of European legislation. This failure to scrutinise European legislation adequately, however, has a deeper effect than merely a failure to spot potential legislative inadequacies.

With the ruthless centralisation of power over the past two decades into the hands of the government and Whitehall, it is hard to retain a belief in the role of Parliament as the voice of the people. Ferdinand Mount in *The British Constitution Now* accurately identifies the dilemma:

> ... It is not simply the unchallengability of ministerial decisions that has come into question. It is the legislative efficacy as well as the dignity of Parliament. It is part of the law of the land that, in areas covered by Community law, that law is superior to British law. But it adds insult to self-inflicted injury that the upstart European Parliament – which stalwart British parliamentarians like Mrs Thatcher have asserted not to be a 'real parliament' at all – should, in fact, be more effective as a scrutineer of European legislation than the British Parliament is of British legislation. A high proportion of Euro-MPs' amendments are incorporated into European legislation; for British Opposition and backbenchers, the proportion of successful amendments is ... extremely small. As for exercising influence over European legislation, we have seen too how disgracefully slow the House of Commons has been to wake up to its responsibilities and opportunities; debates have been held in the small hours, attended only by a handful of fanatics, and often timed too late in any case to affect the UK government's negotiating position.

So what is it exactly that Sir James and his allies want? Is it, perhaps, that despite his belief in "local and participatory" democracy, he believes it is acceptable that power should remain in the hands of certain political elites, provided that they are national elites? Surely, the way the British Parliament presently handles European legislation hardly inspires confidence.

It is difficult to understand exactly what is being defended with such tenacity except, perhaps, the privileges and diminishing status of MPs who are all too aware of their declining reputation with their electorates and are seeking scapegoats on whom to load the opprobrium.

About what he calls the "unelected technocrats" of the Commission, Sir James writes:

> Originally power had been entrusted to the Council of Ministers, which consists of the elected national heads of state or their representatives. As they were more interested in national policies than in the creation of Europe, bit by bit [the unelected technocrats] were allowed to take over executive power. They have been granted the monopoly right to propose new initiatives for the development of the European Union.

This is a gross misreading of the treaties. It was the intention of the founders of the European Union from the very beginning to give the Commission the sole right to initiate legislation as a way of driving forward the process of integration. But the right to initiate legislation only begins the process. The power to *decide* legislation remains with the Council of Ministers, although it is increasingly shared with the EP.

That was always the case. The Council of Ministers has never enjoyed an unbridled exercise of power. Furthermore, the European Council, which is the body consisting of Prime Ministers and Heads of State, only came into being officially with the Maastricht Treaty. It does indeed set the agenda for the Union's legislative and executive activities but it is a *separate* institution from the Council of

77

Ministers. The Council of Ministers refers to the several Councils in which sit Ministers appropriate to the subject under discussion. Few Heads of State are elected – the British monarch is not one of them – and unless several constitutions have been re-written, Ministers are not usually considered to be the 'representatives' of Heads of State. They are, presumably, accountable to their home parliaments. Sir James is fluent but not always accurate.

What is disturbing about Sir James's analysis is not so much the mistakes he makes but that, underlying his thesis, one sees no desire to devolve power but rather a desire to keep it in the hands of the national elites. If this *is* the intention of the Referendum Party, then it should be more clearly spelt out. Behind his call for a referendum hides a call to defend the *status quo*, perhaps even to set the clock back.

Unfortunately, what many of these and other similarly 'sceptical' arguments have done is to distract public attention from the central issue which is not how to remove the European level of government, but rather how to reform it. And, as Former Foreign Minister Douglas Hurd suggested in a *Sunday Times* article on 19 May 1996: "It is hard to encourage Brussels to more energetic effort if the background noises from Britain suggest this is an institution we are trying not to reform but to destroy."

9. The need for a sense of direction

Although the terms of reference of the IGC offer the opportunity to examine a wide area of options, it is unlikely that any changes recommended will involve radical reshaping of the existing institutions. The essential task will be to find the right balance between those institutions which have been created to represent Europe and its citizens directly – the Commission, the EP and the Court of Justice – and those which represent the member states – the Council of Ministers and the European Council. Like any structures which share power, there is a tension between them both in practical and philosophical terms. The EP claims, as the only body directly elected by European citizens, to speak exclusively on their behalf. On the other hand, the Council of Ministers and the European Council claim the authority of national sovereignty and the democratic legitimacy of national elections.

Which has the better case depends on your political views. But, as we have seen, national parliaments, as opposed to national governments, have very little say in the way European legislation is negotiated and passed at the moment, . Firstly, parliamentary timetables are usually overflowing with national legislation; secondly, MPs are rarely consulted in advance about European legislation; and, finally, they are in the difficult position of being presented with a decision which, having taken weeks or months to negotiate, is difficult to alter without reopening the entire debate. If European legislation is to be properly scrutinised, a supra-national parliament seems necessary to do the job.

Two questions that need to be answered are how to ensure that citizens have the greatest possible control over their lives at every level of the Union. And how can this be accomplished within the context of the Union's membership doubling over the next one or two decades?

Giving the EP the power of co-decision in all areas of legislation would increase the democracy of the institutions but, by itself, would not entirely answer the underlying question of how far the Europe Union needs a recognised and identifiable government. At present, it is governed by institutions both federal and inter-governmental but those institutions do not make a government. That is the heart of the confusion for many people.

At the national level, people can vote out politicians who make decisions they dislike. At the European level this is not possible for no one institution is directly responsible. The antis may claim that this is precisely their argument and justifies their case for sweeping away the present institutions and making European decisions by inter-governmental means. But they are wrong. As we have already discussed, this does not solve the problem. Not only are national parliaments unable to scrutinise legislation satisfactorily, but, if every piece of European legislation was to require the express approval of thirty national parliaments, the whole process would grind to a halt.

The answer lies in ensuring that the citizen can be represented adequately at every level of government and can exercise the ultimate sanction of removing those decision-makers with whom they are dissatisfied. But to remove an unpopular or inadequate government implies that there is a government in the first place. How could this be achieved at the European level?

There are, of course, a number of models which could be used as a theoretical basis for constructing a European government. Federalism does not offer one single solution but a set of guiding principles. The two most obvious examples of federal government, practised in many parts of the world, are the parliamentary and the presidential systems.

In the parliamentary model, the legislative power of the Union would rest with one or more parliamentary chambers at least one of which would be directly elected by the citizens of Europe. A second could be elected either as a senate representing the member states, or on a regional basis, or it could be appointed by national parliaments from among their own members.

In such a system, the executive would be elected by the Parliament, probably from their own membership, on European party lines. The executive would be accountable to the Parliament and could be removed by it. Elections would be for a fixed term and conducted on a Europe-wide basis under a uniform proportional system.

The respective powers and competencies of the legislature, the executive and an independent judiciary would be laid down in a constitution which could be ratified both by national parliaments and, perhaps, by referenda throughout the Union.

The advantages of the parliamentary model include its simplicity, the directness of its procedures and the clarity of its democracy.

Its main disadvantage, however, is that it presumes a degree of political integration and a rejection of national governments that is far beyond anything that would be acceptable in today's Europe. Even with a well-drafted constitution, it would be naive to suppose that an EP and an executive with that degree of authority would not usurp powers that are the prerogative of the nation state. The ultimate danger is that it could lead to a voluntary federation becoming a coercive federation.

The presidential model allows for greater checks and balances than the parliamentary system. The essential element in the presidential system is the direct election by all the people of Europe of either an individual President who could then choose other members of his or her team in a number of different ways, or of a full Commission (or executive body).

Such a directly elected Commission would have the right to initiate legislation either exclusively or as a shared right with the Parliament.

The Parliament would be directly elected on a uniform electoral basis and could consist of one or more chambers, elected in one of the ways suggested under the parliamentary model. It would have the power to initiate and approve legislation.

An independent judiciary would interpret the constitution and settle disputes arising under the Union's laws. In other words, the European Union would begin to look a little like the United States.

The problem with the presidential model, as with the parliamentary, is that it is unlikely that either solution would be strong enough to avoid a progressive erosion of states' rights and the strengthening of the federal authorities. Even with a second chamber directly representing the member states, it is unlikely that centripetal forces could be resisted.

Although neither system is entirely appropriate to Europe's needs at the present time, and such grand designs do not fall within the terms of reference of the IGC, it is perhaps time that some aspects of both forms of government should be openly examined for their relevance in solving the Union's problems, which are in essence: how can institutions set up to integrate six countries, cope efficiently with a possible membership of up to thirty countries, while, at the same time, finding a way to increase the Union's democratic legitimacy?

I have no doubt that the suggestion will meet with fierce opposition. The idea that the governance of the Union should be so clearly defined and the institutions placed within a recognisable constitutional framework will horrify not just the Union's opponents but many of its most active supporters who prefer a *sui generis* approach that does not carry the burden of defining an end product. But, without a clear idea of where the Union is heading, not only will it be difficult to find lasting solutions to increasingly complex problems but any solutions that are found will further increase public confusion and uncertainty. Whatever their merits, however, these broader issues are not within the IGC's terms of reference. It has set itself a much more limited task, though in the Reflection Group's report there are hopeful signs that some of the central issues will be considered.

Because of the complexity of institutional reform and the profound disagreements between member states which emerged in the Reflection Group, no consensus was established and a number of alternatives remain to be considered. On some issues, however, there was agreement, for instance:

- that no new institutions should be created. Though seemingly innocuous, this was an interesting decision as it precluded the idea that national parliaments should be represented in a separate chamber,

- that, as far as possible, there should be a move towards one single institutional framework, rather than three separate pillars,

- that the existing institutional balance between the 'European' and the inter-governmental institutions should be maintained,

- that the Union must preserve its ability to make decisions when it has up to 30 members.

10. Institutional reform: the Parliament and the Council

The complexity of decision-making in the EU and the prospect of further enlargement raise various problems which should be considered at the IGC. With the possibility, after enlargement, of a further hundred million voters, how large should the Parliament become? To go to 1,000 members would make debate impossible. To make it too small would lead to vast constituencies. The solution recommended by the Reflection Group was to limit the size to 700 members (a little larger that the UK parliament). As existing member states will have fewer MEPs than at present, this will mean redrawing the boundaries of existing Euro-seats in the UK. Other member states may seek different solutions.

Are there presently too many decision-making procedures? If the EP were restricted to just three: co-decision (with the Council of Ministers), assent and consultation, there would be little effect on the exiting institutional balance.

The key question is: should the EP have the right of co-decision with the Council of Ministers in every area of Community legislation? Those who favour this idea argue that, as the only directly elected institution in the European Community, the EP should be a full partner in agreeing European legislation. After all, MEPs are answerable directly to their electors while the Council of Ministers is only indirectly answerable to the electorate through national parliaments, which may not have the time or the inclination to discover the facts or fully understand the arguments.

The opposing argument is that the EP needs first to demonstrate that it is an effective institution for dealing with the limited powers it already possesses before these are extended. Indeed, the strongest defenders of national sovereignty in European decision-making not only oppose any attempt whatsoever to extend the Parliament's powers but would prefer to see them reduced.

Although it is likely that the majority opinion in the IGC will be in favour of extending the Parliament's powers and simplifying the co-decision procedures which are cumbersome and complicated, a minority opinion, led by the present British government, will oppose any extension of the Parliament's powers.

At present, the EP must give its agreement to the European Community's overall budget but has less control than the Council of Ministers over the so-called 'compulsory expenditure', i.e. mainly agricultural expenditure. Should MEPs be given more control over this part of the budget where, it must be said, the Council of Minister's performance has left much to be desired?

While bearing in mind the distinction between the powers exercised by the Commission in enforcing the Community's decisions and those exercised by the national governments, there was considerable support for increasing the powers of the EP and the Ombudsman to combat fraud and monitor the Commission.

Again, bearing in mind the role of MEPs as the direct representatives of Europe's citizens, should their assent be required on those key matters, such as Treaty changes, agreements with third countries not in the European Union and any increase in the European Union's own resources and revenue which require unanimity in the Council of Ministers?

There is also the major question of what role the EP should play in the election of the Commission. Here too, there are a number of options. At present, Commissioners are appointed by the governments of the member states and are then subject to approval, as a team, by the EP, which can question them individually, but only affirm or reject their appointment, or sack them, collectively. In real terms, this severely limits the chances of the EP influencing the composition of the Commission.

A different formula might be for the EP to elect the President of the Commission directly from a list submitted by the European Council. Once elected, the President would then be free to choose his or her own Commissioners respecting the necessary balance between member states.

Another system would be for the major political groups to propose teams of Commissioners which would then be put before the EP for election. Such a procedure would, of course, take the whole process much closer to the idea of a European government directly answerable to an EP.

The likelihood is that the present system will not be greatly changed, although the Parliament might be given greater powers to challenge individual Commissioners and call them to account.

Finally, a number of groups have drawn attention to the European Parliament's duty, under the Treaty of Rome, to decide upon a uniform electoral system throughout the whole of the European Union for European Parliamentary elections. Although the UK remains the most glaring example – it is the only member state that does not, except in Northern Ireland, use some form of proportional representation – there are also differences between other member states over which type of proportional representation should be used. The EP itself appears ready to accommodate various forms within the overall system.

One of the pitfalls in discussing the division of powers within the European Union has been the tendency to focus on the division of power between European institutions on the one hand, and the governments of the member states on the other. Squeezed between the two are the national parliaments whose role has often been undermined. Although useful work has been undertaken by a joint conference composed of representatives of the European affairs committees of the national parliaments plus a delegation from the EP, this has not really dealt with the alienation many national parliamentarians have felt from the development of European integration. One of the questions asked by the Reflection Group, therefore, was how can national parliaments be more involved?

One solution would be to invite representatives of the national parliaments to form a legislative chamber, in the way that the US Senate represented American states' legislatures before 1913. In this way, the nations of Europe would be represented by their national parliamentarians in one chamber while the people would continue to be represented directly through the EP. A third chamber, alongside the Parliament and the Council of Ministers, would only make the system yet more cumbersome and complex. Yet if the new chamber were to replace the Council, it could be argued that it would greatly increase the democratic legitimacy of Europe, bring decision-making closer to the citizens and therefore increase accountability. The counter-argument is that it would fundamentally change the balance between the inter-governmental and the federal structures and move Europe swiftly towards becoming one country rather than a Union of member states.

Whether or not such an idea evolves in the future, it has been specifically excluded from the agenda of the forthcoming IGC by the Reflection Group.

Instead, the discussions will concentrate on the process by which national parliaments will be able to play a greater role by being better informed and consulted earlier. One concrete suggestion was that national parliaments should receive clear and complete documentation in the relevant official language four weeks before each and every substantial Commission legislative proposal so as to increase opportunities for a full discussion.

How this could be integrated into national parliamentary timetables might pose problems, but it is a significant way not only of bringing national parliaments more closely into the debate but also increasing dramatically the accountability of ministers in the various Councils. On the issue of accountability, the question may also be raised as to whether European Commissioners should be invited, or indeed compelled, to appear before national parliaments.

With the growing need for strategic leadership in Europe, and an increase, under the Maastricht Treaty, of inter-governmental co-operation in key areas, the role of the European Council has grown significantly.

As the European Union faces up to further enlargement, however, both the European Council and the Council of Ministers will require substantial reform. The qualified majority voting procedures have speeded up decision-making, but only in some areas. In others, unanimity is still required. Reform is needed if enlargement is to take place.

Unfortunately, any reform goes to the very heart of the debate about national sovereignty. If, as is suggested, qualified majority voting must be extended to increase efficiency, indeed to make decision-making possible, the right of a member state to use the veto correspondingly diminishes – an idea resolutely opposed by both 'Eurosceptics' and some national governments. On the other hand, extending the veto to twenty or more countries could work on occasions against the interests of all member states.

At the same time, it is clear that the secrecy and lack of scrutiny of both the Council of Ministers and the European Council flies in the face of popular demands for greater transparency and accountability. Unfortunately, with decisions at the IGC in the hands of the European Council, hopes for reform should not be raised too high.

The Reflection Group considered four main areas of reform of the European Council and the Council of Ministers: firstly, the balance between qualified majority voting and the use of the veto especially after further enlargement; secondly, changes in the system of qualified majority voting; thirdly, changes in the Presidency of the Council; and finally, the need for greater scrutiny and the dangers of overlapping with the other institutions.

Inter alia, the Reflection Group considered the following aspects of Council voting procedures:

- whether there should be a tighter definition of issues requiring unanimity in the Council. For example, should new treaties and primary law, accession of new member states, and establishing and changing the way the Union receives its financial resources require no only unanimity but also ratification by national parliaments?

- whether on other issues, the Council should accept the use of qualified majority voting,

- whether a compromise could be that the Council could choose to move to a simpler procedure in certain circumstances, or whether areas which require unanimity, and therefore allow countries to retain their veto, should be set out in the Treaty.

The other major issue concerning qualified majority voting is whether, as it currently stands, it provides the right balance between the size of countries and the size of their populations. The system was devised to ensure that neither the larger not the smaller countries could form a block to outvote the other. However, this can result in majority decisions which represent a qualified majority of countries but not necessarily a majority of the people of Europe as a whole.

One solution would be to link the number of votes a country is given to the size of its population but that could mean very small countries with such a miniscule number of votes that their status as a member state would be undermined.

An alternative could be to require, for certain key areas of legislation, a double majority consisting of four-fifths of all the member states plus four-fifths of the populations of the EU. Some people have suggested that this should replace unanimity in certain key areas, but it does not meet the arguments of those who feel a national veto should remain on principle.

At present, each member state holds the Presidency of the Union for six months in rotation. When there were twelve members, this meant once every six years; with fifteen, it becomes every seven and a half years; with 24, countries will need to wait twelve years – often two or three political generations. There are no simple solutions to this problems, but suggestions include:

- regionalising the Presidency. In other words, perhaps an Iberian or a Nordic Presidency could be followed by one from the Benelux countries or Central and Eastern Europe. The larger countries would assume the role on their own. Of course, this solution also throws up some obvious problems: some countries, such as Ireland do not have any obvious neighbours with whom to share the presidency. It also implies that a regional grouping would necessarily share common objectives, which might not be the case.

- the election by the European Council, and perhaps the European Parliament, of an individual, chosen on merit, to act as President on their behalf. One problem might be how to balance the authority which would come from such an election with the existing authority of the Presidents of the Commission and Parliament.

- the creation of a team system with four Presidents, one among them being *primus inter pares*, acting for twelve months rather than the present six months.

The Reflection Group reached no conclusions on this issue.

In order to deal with the question of greater accountability, there is a widespread and growing belief that the time has come for the Council of Ministers to open its proceedings to public scrutiny both by increasing access to its minutes (which it has done in a limited way since 1995) and allowing press and media reporting, at least of the vote, if not of the full debate.

One problem which arises is that a distinction may have to be drawn between the Council of Ministers' role as a law maker, which, like the Parliament, requires openness, scrutiny and responsibility, and its executive decisions, which like, a cabinet, require a certain privacy. Another is that by allowing the full debate to be reported, there is a real danger that a minister's room for compromise would be severely reduced as unwarranted press and media pressure might influence the scope of the negotiations.

Although it is important that the Council of Ministers is well served by its own staff who prepare much of the work in advance of the meetings, there is always the danger both of a proliferation of committees and that the work of the Council and its civil servants will overlap with that of the Commission. Indeed, 'comitology', the system of Commission chaired committees (legislative, regulatory and advisory) which operate in secret and without any parliamentary presence, not only hinders the cause of openness but can both confuse and irritate the public.

Not surprisingly, the Reflection Group reached no conclusions on many of these issues. The IGC itself will find it equally difficult. Not only do they challenge may of the false preconceptions currently held about the nature of the Union but their solution will require a compromise about its future direction that may prove very hard to find.

11. Institutional Reform: the Commission and the Court

The Commission is unquestionably the institution that the press most loves to hate. And, at times, a certain irritation can enter into the soul of even the most enthusiastic European who has to deal with the Commission first hand; for example, its payment of Community grants is notoriously slow and bureaucratic. Yet its powers are usually wildly exaggerated and its mistakes often unfairly magnified. If it has been accused of excessive zeal in making proposals which constitute unjustifiable interference in what many deem to be the prerogative of the nation state, this is because it has, like all organisations, used its designated authority to the full. But it has rarely exceeded its powers and is surprisingly open and approachable.

Although its powers are clear and limited – proposing legislation, carrying out legislation which has been agreed by the Council and, where there is co-decision, the Parliament, and enforcing compliance – its political position is more confused. It has some governmental powers such as the right to initiate legislation and to negotiate internationally in certain circumstances such as the GATT talks. But it is not a government and is ultimately subject, to the authority of both the Parliament and the European Council. At the same time, it is certainly more than just a civil service. This uncertainty makes its task extremely difficult and its role confusing to the general public.

Commissioners may speak out on public, political matters in a way that no civil servant could, yet they have no direct political constituency. Quite how long this delicate balancing act can be maintained is uncertain but it will depend, in the long run, on whether the Commission is destined to move towards assuming a greater governmental role and accountability to the EP, or lose some of its political authority as Europe moves towards a more inter-governmental system.

Meanwhile, the issues that are likely to be on the agenda of the IGC divide into two main groups – the competencies of the Commission and its structures.

Unlike most parliaments, the EP does not have the power to introduce legislation itself although, since Maastricht, the EP can invite the Commission to put forward legislation in any field of European Union competence. Many MEPs, however, believe that it should be given the power to introduce legislation, either as an automatic right, or in cases where the Commission refuses to introduce legislation after a certain length of time.

In its proposals, the Reflection Group rejects that proposal and reaffirms a belief that the Commission should be the only institution with the right to propose legislation.

Similarly, despite some uneasiness on the part of member states that the Commission is becoming involved in too many areas of activity – the so-called 'nooks and crannies' argument – it is unlikely that the IGC will greatly alter the Commission's present system of responsibilities. Nevertheless, among the questions that are likely to be examined are:

- how much executive power should rest with the Commission and how much should be exercised jointly with the Council? Should the Commission have a greater or lesser executive role?
- how much of the implementation of the Community's legislation should rest with the Commission and how much with the member states?
- should the Commission produce an annual report on the implementation of legislation?
- should private individuals have more effective means of action to appeal against national governments' failure to comply with Community legislation?
- should the Commission and, by implication, the Community as a whole do not more but better? Or should its work be expanded to include important areas that might benefit from greater coordination like tourism or energy?

Much more consideration will be given to how the Commission will cope with the challenge of enlargement.

At present, there are twenty Commissioners, with only the five larger member states – France, Germany, Italy, Spain and the UK – allowed two each. Every other member state has one Commissioner. If twelve more member states, including the Visegrad and Baltic countries, Bulgaria, Romania and Slovenia as well as Malta and Cyprus were to join, with only one new member – Poland – entitled to two Commissioners, the number would rise to 33. Already, the portfolios have had to be subdivided to provide jobs for twenty Commissioners, a further subdivision would be unrealistic.

A number of alternatives have been suggested including:

* the idea that all member states should be allowed one Commissioner only. Although this might be a temporary solution, there would also be the problem that Germany with 80 million people and Luxembourg with 350,000 would be equally represented. A solution might be to introduce qualified majority voting into the Commission. Many, however, believe this would be cumbersome and undermine the collective or 'collegiate' feeling of the Commission.

* the view that there should be senior and junior Commissioners, with most large states having at least one permanent senior Commissioner, and the junior Commissioners rotating duties?

* the point that the President of the Commission should be appointed by the Council or elected by the Parliament and then left to pick his or her team from lists supplied by the member states, according to broad geographical guidelines.

The Reflection Group stressed that it was important that all the Commissioners should be properly qualified and independent from their country's interests.

There are two questions here: whether the Commission should be made more accountable and, if so, to whom? Predictably, it divides between those in favour of greater accountability to the EP (likely to be a majority of the IGC) and those in favour of greater accountability to the Council (supporters of inter-governmentalism.) An associated issue is whether the Commission should continue to exercise powers jointly with the Council or move to a greater or lesser executive role.

In recent months, those opposed to further European integration have increasingly focused their attacks upon the ECJ. As it is called upon both to determine the legitimacy of Community legislation as well as to interpret it and to settle disputes, the ECJ increasingly resembles a Supreme Court. Certainly, it has the authority to overrule, within the areas of its jurisdiction, the highest courts of the member states, including the British House of Lords.

The ECJ's role, perhaps more clearly than that of any other institution, highlights the federal nature of the European Union. At its simplest, the underlying question that the IGC must face is: should the ECJ be strengthened to ensure uniform interpretation of and compliance to Community law or is this taking us down the road to federalism? To take the negative view would severely diminish its ability to enforce Community legislation including the laws that make the single market, whereas to enhance its powers increasingly puts member states under a legal obligation more usually associated with the federal state.

Apart from the major issues of principle, some important practical questions will need to be answered by the IGC, including:

*   should the ECJ's role in Justice and Home Affairs be increased so that it can ensure compliance with human and civil rights legislation?
*   should the Court have the ability to enforce penalties more swiftly and should it speed up its procedures?
*   are the ECJ judgements sometimes disproportionate in their effect? Should there be limits to member states' economic liability if they have genuinely tried to comply and should there be time limits on retrospective judgements and a right of appeal?

- should appointments of Judges be extended to nine years with no possibility of reappointment?

- as the problem of numbers after enlargement arises again, should each member state continue to have a Judge or should the total be made up between Judges and Advocates General?

- should the European Court be assisted by regional courts, or would that interfere with the exercise of justice in the member states?

As well as the four main institutions, the IGC will need to examine the work of other, extremely important organs and processes of the Union if they are to be reformed and brought into line with new demands and needs that have arisen.

12. Foreign affairs

The Union's willingness and ability to take common action on the international scene will be a major issue on the table at the IGC. This in turn divides into two broad areas:

- its economic relations with the rest of the world
- its foreign and security policy.

Putting these two issues together under the general heading of 'external action' focuses immediately on one problem – that the decision-making procedures for the European Union's external economic relations are not only different from those for common foreign and security policy (CFSP) but the two actually fall within different 'pillars' of the Union. Not surprisingly, this leads to some confusion in both theory and practice.

Most economic policy decisions fall within the scope of the single market legislation and are made using the procedures and institutions of the European Community – the Commission, the Council and the EP. It is an area of notable achievement, particularly the GATT agreements on world trade at which the European Union, represented by the Commission, gained considerable advantage by negotiating collectively.

But, while it has been accepted that the European Community should play a leading role in representing the member states in economic affairs, the same is not yet true of foreign and security policy or defence. On single market issues, the EP can exercise co-decision, but not on foreign and security policy. Indeed, one problem is the confusion that arises as the two areas impinge one upon the other as, for example, in the highly charged issue of arms sales.

Like other 'big' issues such as the reform of the institutions and Justice and Home Affairs, the whole question of whether defence, security and foreign policy decisions should be made by individual countries or the Union as a whole will be fiercely contested.

On the surface, it would seem that the debate should be about what system can best guarantee long term peace and security in Europe and enable the member states of the European Union to defend themselves against external aggression. Underneath, however, is the far more emotive issue of how much a nation's sovereignty depends upon its ability to act independently in pursuing foreign policy objectives and whether the rest of the world recognises it as a separate and individual entity.

Placing member states' defence capabilities under the Union's authority would challenge traditional ideas about national identity. It would also remove forever the usual way European nations have settled their disputes, namely going to war. While this would appear to be an unrestricted benefit, the reality is not quite so straightforward.

The rise of nation states has been inextricably linked with war. Determining national frontiers inevitably led to conflict with neighbouring states and feelings of national unity were strengthened – and not infrequently manipulated – by the threat of external aggression.

Logically, removing the threat to peace and security should lead to an overwhelming sense of relief. Unfortunately, it can also lead to exactly the opposite: feelings of uncertainty and fear. It is not easy to replace traditional suspicions with a sense of trust and mutual understanding.

For some member states, especially France and the UK, two of the oldest nation states in the world, there will be a reluctance to allow foreign and security, let alone defence, policies to be further merged into the Union's decision-making processes. For others, it is the surest way to make Europe safe and effective as it approaches the new millennium.

A major debate is likely to emerge concerning whether CSFP (and Justice and Home Affairs) should remain as separate pillars of the EU, or whether both should be placed under the decision-making processes of the European Community.

Although there are both procedural and political differences in the treatment of CFSP on the one hand and defence policy decision-making on the other – defence policy is about the control of armed forces and their operational deployment in time of war – they are intimately connected. The failure to establish effective security structures can lead to the need for military defence, and both fall within the context of foreign policy. In order to simplify this description, they will be examined together except where specific decisions relate to them separately.

The whole issue is further complicated by the overlap between the role of the European Union and that of other groupings and alliances such as the North Atlantic Treaty Organisation (NATO), Western European Union (WEU) and the Organisation for Security and Cooperation in Europe (OSCE).

To simplify matters, I shall firstly define the role of these various organisations and how they relate to each other, then examine the new problems presently confronting them and, finally, look at some of the suggested solutions that will be discussed at the IGC.

The four key institutions involved in foreign, security and defence policy decision-making in Europe are: the European Union (through the CFSP), the North Atlantic Treaty Organisation, the Western European Union, the Organisation for Security and Cooperation in Europe.

Common Foreign and Security Policy

CFSP became the second pillar of the European Union through the Maastricht Treaty. There had been common policies before, but the Treaty went further, setting out certain key objectives:

- safeguarding the common values, fundamental interests and independence of the European Union,

- strengthening the security of the Union and its member states,

- preserving the peace and strengthening international security in accordance with the United Nations Charter and the Helsinki Act (which created the Conference – now the Organisation – on Security and Cooperation in Europe),

- promoting international cooperation, and
- developing and consolidating democracy and the rule of law, and respect for human rights and fundamental freedoms.

The aim of these limited objectives was to allow the European Union to assert its identity on the international scene. In other words to play a part which was proportional to its size and economic strength. In order to keep the decision-making process firmly in the hands of the member states, however, a separate pillar was created within which the governments of the member states would be firmly in the saddle and the Commission's role would be largely consultative.

The European Council defines the general policy guidelines and, where necessary, the Council of Ministers – in this case Foreign or Defence Ministers – can take common positions and decide whether or not to take joint action. When a common position is taken, member states must ensure that their national policies conform to it. The Council of Ministers normally takes decisions unanimously but can define those matters where qualified majority voting may be used. In other words, they must agree unanimously as to which decisions they can take with qualified majority voting.

The European Commission and EP are not formally part of the decision-making process unless the Council of Ministers chooses to involve them. Nevertheless, the Commission may refer questions on foreign and security policy matters to the Council of Ministers. The EP may be consulted, can put questions and recommendations to the Council and holds an annual debate on the progress towards implementing common policies.

In an emergency, a meeting of the Council of Ministers can be called within 48 hours and the President of the Council (whichever country has the Presidency of the Community for that six months) is responsible for ensuring that policy is carried out. The Treaty also makes it quite clear that the new procedures will not prejudice the specific defence and security policies of individual member states in NATO and it strengthens the operational role of the Western European Union.

North Atlantic Treaty Organisation

NATO was formed in 1949 to provide for a defensive military and political alliance between initially twelve and now 16 nations, some, but not all, of whom are in the European Union.

The present membership consists of Belgium, Canada, Denmark, France, Germany, Greece, Iceland, Italy, Luxembourg, the Netherlands, Norway, Portugal, Spain, Turkey, the UK and the USA.

Between its formation and 1989, its principal role was to defend its members against potential communist aggression. Since the collapse of communism in Europe and the emergence of the new democracies in Central and Eastern Europe, its tasks have become more complex and its role harder to define with precision.

Events in the former Yugoslavia – a portent of what may take place elsewhere – have given it new work to do providing tactical military sanctions within the framework of the greater peace-keeping strategy of the United Nations. But, although it has adapted its structures to meet the security challenges of the new Europe, including peacekeeping operations, it still remains the main defensive organisation for all its members.

NATO's political authority derives from the North Atlantic Council chaired by the Secretary General, presently a Spaniard, which is the highest authority of the Alliance and is composed of permanent representatives from the sixteen member states. There is also a Defence Planning Committee, composed of representatives of each member state except France, and a Nuclear Planning Group. All its decisions have to be agreed unanimously.

The senior military authority is the Military Committee composed of the Chiefs of Defence staff of each member state. Since 1995, it has a Rapid Reaction Corps, a main defence force and augmentation forces of reserves and territorials.

Since 1991, in response to the desire for closer cooperation between the members of the Alliance and the states of Central and Eastern Europe and the former Soviet Union, a North Atlantic Cooperation

Council (NACC) has been formed to facilitate official and informal ties on defence and security matters. In 1994, the bridge building process was taken further with the launch of the Partnership for Peace Programme which offered the new democracies of Central and Eastern Europe and the former Soviet Union a gradual path towards full membership of NATO.

Western European Union

The WEU began life in 1948 as the Brussels Pact, and was intended to provide a form of common defence and economic, social and cultural collaboration amongst its members which include, at present, Belgium, France, Germany, Greece, Italy, Luxembourg, the Netherlands, Portugal, Spain and the UK.

With the formation of NATO, the Council of Europe and then the European Community the importance of the Western European Union diminished considerably. For many years, it continued primarily as a useful forum for discussion, especially with France whose relations with NATO were extremely frosty until comparatively recently.

Since the Maastricht Treaty, however, its role has been considerably revitalised as the organisation that could potentially take the lead in creating a unified European defence structure. The operational role of the WEU was strengthened, with a planning cell, closer military cooperation, regular meetings of the Chiefs of Defence Staff and more cooperation in the armaments field with the aim of creating a European armaments agency.

A key question has been whether the WEU itself should be developed as a European defence arm or whether it should be incorporated eventually into the European Union and, even more radically, placed under the control of the Community's institutions.

The British view, as set out forcibly by John Major in February 1996, is that the WEU's political structures should remain intergovernmental but that it should become 'operationally capable' of running military operations and undertake humanitarian, peacekeeping and crisis management as soon as possible.

Organisation on Security and Cooperation in Europe

Originally called the Conference on Security and Cooperation in Europe (CSCE), the Organisation on Security and Coperation in Europe (OSCE) was established by a Treaty signed in Helsinki in 1975 by members of NATO and the Warsaw Pact and by neutral and non-aligned European countries. It set out several agreements designed to further security and cooperation between all European nations in a number of areas including science and technology and the environment and set out some important humanitarian guidelines.

After 1989, the CSCE was seen by many as the key organisation to promote security and develop peaceful methods of conflict resolution in Europe. With membership covering the whole of Europe and beyond, the renamed OSCE should be well placed to assist member states in developing democratic structures and in finding ways to preempt conflict. What it cannot do, however, is to enforce decisions or agreements reached with its assistance: it has no military competence whatsoever.

Unfortunately, none of these structures, with the exception of NATO, was able to play a significant role in the former Yugoslavia and most particularly Bosnia. The European Union failed to guarantee peace and security even in its own 'back yard'. If peace lasts, most of the credit will go the USA whose direct involvement, including a willingness to use military sanctions and the hosting of intense negotiations in Dayton, Ohio, seems to have resulted in, at the very least, a prolonged ceasefire and perhaps lasting stability in the region.

In fairness, although it failed to prevent conflict or directly broker peace, Western Europe played the major role in providing both peacekeeping forces on the ground through the United Nations and humanitarian relief. Nevertheless, the Common Foreign and Security Policy of the European Union has emerged without glory or any coherent policies as to how to deal with similar problems should they occur in the future.

Indeed, if Europe is faced with similar problems in the future, it will have to decide whether it can safely, or indeed morally, ignore them or whether it will need to take considerably swifter and more effective measures. If it decides to act, will it need to become more united in its foreign and security policy decision-making? If the answer is 'yes', then does that necessarily mean that CFSP should be included within the European Community's institutional framework or are there other alternatives including strengthening the operational role of the Western European Union? Indeed, are these options mutually exclusive in the long run?

One fundamental disagreement is between those who believe that collective responsibility should be deepened by involving the other key European institutions – the Commission and the EP – in foreign affairs, and those who wish to see decision-making on defence matters remain within the WEU, separate from the European Union. Another is between those who want the WEU to have a real capacity including, for example, a rapid reaction force, and those who do not.

If a greater role were given to the Western European Union, including the possibility of taking direct military action, it might, in a sense, become the European arm of NATO. One problem with this suggestion, however, is that the European membership of the Western European Union and that of NATO are not the same. Some European Union member states, for example Austria, Finland, Ireland and Sweden, are neutral.

What would happen if there were a disagreement between the two organisations or if some EU members did not wish to take part in joint actions?

The relationship between the Western European Union and NATO is clearly crucial and a great deal of effort has been directed towards greater coordination between the two bodies. Although, at the moment, the Western European Union's role is primarily humanitarian, peacekeeping and peacemaking in nature, NATO has supported the idea of the Western European Union taking a greater defence role and endorsed the idea of combined joint task forces. In order to develop the relationship further, the Western European Union has moved its headquarters to Brussels, the main home of the European Community's institutions and also of NATO, and a number of joint NATO-WEU committees have been created.

The position of neutral countries, or indeed member states who do not want to take part in activities that are not directly related to defence, is a crucial issue. The most likely solution, which has been endorsed by the Reflection Group, is that while member states not wishing to participate in an activity should not be compelled to do so, neither should they be allowed to prevent the other member states from taking action.

For example, should a majority of member states agree to contribute forces or logistical support to a future conflict, like the Gulf War, the minority who did not wish to take part would not be coerced into doing so but neither would they be able to prevent European involvement, even if there were future economic, or indeed military, repercussions.

This would remain true whether defence policy decisions remained inter-governmental, as is now the case and as it is in the Western European Union, or became fully integrated into the European Community's institutional framework.

Those who wish to see defence policy fully integrated into the Union's institutional structure offer three main reasons:

- that it would enhance the ability of the Union to play a part in world events commensurate with its size and economic strength;

- that it would allow the European Parliament to be involved in crucial decisions of war or peace that would put the lives of European citizens at risk, and

- that it would remove the anomaly whereby the Union's external economic decisions are taken by one procedure, CFSP by another, and defence decisions differently again.

A further key issue is how to react to the desire of Central and Eastern European countries and, indeed, the former Soviet Union, who wish to become part of a European defence alliance.

As we saw earlier, NATO has begun the task of finding ways to integrate formerly hostile forces into the Western alliance. Unfortunately, the process is complicated on the one hand by the desire of the Central and Eastern European countries, which continue to harbour suspicions about the intentions of the Russian Federation, to speed up the process of integration, and on the other the Russian Federation, which fears that this may lead to a new sense of isolation at a time when greater trust is required.

The European Union is also conscious that in extending its frontiers eastwards it may inherit unresolved conflicts with which it would be required to deal.

Although these are complex issues that cannot be resolved directly at this IGC, they will form a background to the discussions that will take place.

The underlying disagreement between those who wish to see CFSP remain a separate pillar and those who wish to see it integrated into the institutions of the Union will surface in many ways but is unlikely to be resolved.

For example, some members felt that there was a need to extend the use of qualified majority voting if any progress was to be made towards effective decision-making. This idea is another way of bringing the decisions within the overall framework of the Community and as such will be opposed by those who believe that the removal of the national veto also removes important aspects of sovereignty.

Compromise solutions were outlined. For example, one way of increasing cooperation might be to establish a CFSP Analysis and Planning Unit recruited from the member states, the Council's secretariat and the Commission but answerable directly to the Council. This Unit could be established within the institutional framework of the European Community and assist with analysis, early warning and planning.

This might well assist the Council to make decisions but it raises several questions. How would it tie in with the work of the WEU? Would the institutions eventually merge? If so, under what framework – inter-governmental or institutional? Should the Head of the Unit be the Secretary General of the Council and could the job be merged with that of the Secretary General of the WEU? Or should there be a new post – a High Representative who can speak on behalf of the Union as a whole on CFSP matters? But, if that were the case, would there not be a proliferation of people speaking for the Union on different issues, creating all the more confusion?

The IGC will thus have to face up to the major task of answering the question once posed by Henry Kissinger when he was US National Security Advisor: "Who is this Europe? If I want to telephone Europe in a crisis, to whom do I speak?"

If it is to have an influence on world affairs, the European Union will need to find a convincing answer.

13. Justice and home affairs

Like Foreign and Security policy, Justice and Home Affairs was placed in a separate pillar of the European Union by the Maastricht Treaty, which means that the issues raised are dealt with on an inter-governmental basis.

Modern crime such as drug trafficking has little respect for frontiers and, has benefited from the free movement of people, goods and capital. There is evidence, for instance, that money from crime syndicates in Russia is 'laundered' in London and Vienna. Combatting crime cannot be contained within national borders and cooperation between police forces worldwide has been steadily growing.

There are serious worries as to whether existing inter-governmental structures are effective in dealing with organised crime and illegal immigration into the Union, and whether the present system, which excludes proper scrutiny by the EP, sufficiently protects basic civil liberties. There is an ever present danger when seeking methods of dealing with crimes such as terrorism, drug trafficking and the exploitation of illegal immigrants, especially across frontiers, that the solutions undermine respect for fundamental freedoms and civil rights.

So far, Europe's response to drug trafficking, for example, has been poor: there has been an absence of either clear objectives or a timetable for achieving them. At the same time, effective ways of protecting citizens from organised crime can clash with important civil rights such as the right to free movement and privacy. There is also always the fear that an all-embracing European computerised record system will finally bring in the age of 'Big Brother'. Partly for that reason, civil libertarians throughout the European Union have challenged the lack of accountability to the EP of important cross-border police powers.

A BRILLIANT CONSPIRACY?

A very different problem but one which also falls under the third pillar is the arrival of political refugees and economic migrants in the EU. The fall of the Berlin Wall, the Balkan conflict and other major upheavals throughout the world have greatly increased the pressure on European states to accept both political refugees and economic migrants. Indeed, there is no clear distinction between the two groups. The response from member states has varied with Germany far in the lead in being prepared to open its doors to refugees. Faced with potential upheavals in North Africa and elsewhere, as well as further moves to remove internal frontiers, there will be increasing pressures on the member states to develop coordinated policies on the control of external borders and the acceptance of refugees and migrants from third countries.

The most radical solution would be to integrate Justice and Home Affairs into the main, first pillar of the Union, hence placing key issues such as immigration policy, asylum for refugees, common rules for external border controls and crime prevention under the control of the Community's institutions – the Commission, the Parliament, the Council and the Court of Justice.

This solution will be fiercely opposed by those who are concerned that the Community is already doing too much and resent what they see as intrusion in this area. The UK Government is against increasing the powers of the Community's institutions as opposed to the inter-governmental structures and will certainly be supported by many other Ministries of Home Affairs. It is, nevertheless, an issue which should arouse widespread public concern and it will continue to be closely monitored by civil liberties groups and organisations concerned with protecting refugees and migrants.

The key will be to find solutions to these problems that are, at the same time, fair, open, accountable and effective – not an easy task!

Even if, as seems likely, the IGC decides to maintain Justice and Home Affairs as a separate pillar, it is worth recalling that the Reflection Group suggested other reforms which might nonetheless be feasible, for example:

- allowing some specific issues – arrangements for aliens, immigration and asylum policy and common rules for external border controls – to be brought under EC control,
- finding ways of working more closely and efficiently with the institutions of the European Community when tasks overlap,
- allowing the European Parliament some rights to propose legislation in this field,
- reducing the use of the veto in the Council of Ministers and extending qualified majority voting in the Council on some justice and home affairs issues except when especially sensitive,
- harmonising national penal codes on fraud,
- establishing a clearer definition of objectives and methods,
- finding ways of working more closely and efficiently with the institutions of the European Community when tasks overlap,
- cooperating more closely with the Council of Europe in the fight against drugs (remembering that new sources of supply have sprung up in Central and Eastern Europe).

In summary: on the question of Justice and Home Affairs, although ways might be found to improve existing mechanisms, there is an almost irresistible case, on the grounds of simplicity, democracy and civil rights, to integrate the third pillar into the European Community as a whole.

Citizenship

It is frequently argued that the question of citizenship should be at the very top of the IGC agenda. Indeed, the think tank set up to prepare the agenda began its report by stressing the central role of European citizenship not just as the source of the Union's democratic legitimacy but also as the key to winning the support of people of Europe.

Certainly, without the support of its citizens, the whole concept of European integration is meaningless, but there is a long way to go yet before most people make the kind of emotional and intellectual attachment to Europe that would compare to their sense of belonging to their own country.

Indeed, it may be the case that the meaning of citizenship at a national level – with all the rights and duties the term implies – will never be replicated at the European level. On the other hand, with an increasing number of decisions that directly affect the day to day life of ordinary people being made at the European level, and with more people working and living abroad, it is crucial that the European Union accepts responsibility for the protection of certain basic rights and offers some additional advantages.

Some of these, like the right of residents to vote in certain elections in countries other than their own, and the opportunity to seek assistance from the embassies and consulates of other member states when travelling in third countries, were included in the Maastricht Treaty.

The current IGC will consider more fundamental changes. For example, whether citizens of the Union are adequately protected by existing legislation including the European Convention on Human Rights. The member states of the European Union have all signed the European Convention on Human Rights and Fundamental Freedoms and can be brought before the European Court of Human Rights if they are accused of violating the Convention. Individual member states are members but the European Union as a whole is not. This could lead to anomalies, for example, what to do if the European Union's institutions infringe the Convention.

At present, the protection of citizens from infringement of their rights by European Union institutions rests with the ECJ, with the European Ombudsman and with the European Parliament's Petitions Committee. The European Court does refer to the principles of the Convention on Human Rights and Fundamental Freedoms in its judgments, but citizens might feel more confident if the Convention itself were incorporated into European Union law. One solution would be for the European Community to sign the Convention.

A number of other options will be discussed, for example:

- whether a Bill of Rights could be included in the Treaty. Perhaps there could be a new preamble setting out the rights and freedoms of all European citizens. On the other hand, would it be relevant to the Union as a whole if individual member states have signed and ratified the Convention?

- the Treaty could be amended to proclaim clearly 'European' values such as equality between the sexes, non-discrimination on grounds of race, religion, sexual orientation, age or disability. It could explicitly condemn racism and xenophobia. This, of course, presumes that there are such things as 'common European values' including a commitment to non-discrimination on ethnic, racial, religious or sexual grounds. But is this the case or should citizenship and human rights legislation be left to the individual member states? Could it be that creating common standards might lower as well as raise some national standards?

A further important, if contentious, issue is: should the Treaty extend the social rights and values introduced under Maastricht? Would this reduce EU competitiveness as a whole and create particular problems for poorer member states or is it necessary to protect the rights of working people throughout the Union?

The IGC will also need to consider:

- the relationship between citizenship of the Union and that of individual member states,

- whether nationals of third countries who are not citizens of a member state could become citizens of the Union directly without having to be first citizens of a member state.

The latter is a contentious issue. With free movement of people, workers and migrants from third countries are free to move within the Union, once they have permission to enter one member state. At the same time, member states differ enormously in what they require from applicants for citizenship. Fundamental human rights apply to all persons within the Union whether they are citizens or not but many resident workers of long-standing face discrimination when trying to move freely between member states.

Ironically, the Schengen Agreement, which seeks to create a free travel zone between participatory member states, imposes greater restrictions including stricter police scrutiny on non-EC nationals. The European Community has attempted to mitigate some of the problems by, for example, promoting legislation to allow children of migrant workers full access to education. But a great deal remains to be done to guarantee that all workers within the Union are adequately protected against actual and potential exploitation.

What should happen if a member state fails to implement fundamental rights? Could its membership of the Union be suspended? Could member states actually be expelled? As yet, no member state has refused to accept the jurisdiction of the European courts but what would be the ultimate sanction if they did?

Should the new treaty contain a right to European Union information for all citizens? There is an enormous difference within the Union between member states like Sweden whose citizens have a right of access to state information up to and including the Prime Minister's correspondence and countries like the UK with very restricted rights of information.

While it could not legislate for individual member states, should the European Union open its own books and minutes to scrutiny? Given the obsessive secrecy of the Council of Ministers at present, it might be a major step towards convincing European citizens that the institution of the European Union offered open and transparent government.

Should the use of passports be abolished within the Union? This is another highly contentious issue especially in the UK which has strongly resisted any attempts to dismantle all border controls. National vetoes still exist in this area and so the issue is extremely unlikely to be included in the final treaty.

Some members of the Reflection Group suggested new ideas:

*   Perhaps citizens should have guaranteed rights to public utilities such as electricity, water, postal services, education, or even telephones. Such an idea would very much test the limits of European powers over those of national governments and will inevitably provoke a heated debate. On the one side, it will be fiercely argued that the provision of public utiltities is entirely the responsibility of national governments and to attempt to enforce guaranteed rights would be a direct infringement of national sovereignty. On the other, it may be asserted that the right, for instance, of access to clean water is of fundamental importance to all citizens.

*   Should the European Union set up a 'peace corps' for humanitarian action and public service along the lines of similar American bodies which send young volunteers to help both in third countries and in inner cities? This is a relatively minor subject but one that might well capture imaginations across the Union.

Employment policies

For many people whose lives have been blighted by unemployment the obsessive concern with the Union's institutions can be both irrelevant and insulting. If it is to succeed in capturing and holding the support of ordinary men and women who feel insecure about their futures, including their job prospects, the European Union must be committed to job creation. Unfortunately, although that may sound straightforward, the reality is far more complex. Those working in the EU institutions, and especially the Commission, are faced with a kind of Hobson's Choice: if they do nothing about unemployment, they are seen as insensitive to what is almost certainly Europe's greatest problem today. On the other hand, if, as they have done, they propose Europe-led solutions, national governments accuse them of interference.

What should they do? Again, this is essentially a question of political choice and goes to the root of the debate about how Europe should be governed. At the most simplistic level: should government – at the European or the national level – spend money to create jobs, or should it merely create a competitive environment by deregulation that allows the business community the maximum freedom to create new jobs?

How those questions are answered goes a long way both to defining how people think about Europe and to explaining their political values. For example, a right-wing 'Eurosceptic' is likely to choose a free-market, national solution while a pro-European social-democratic solution might well favour a co-ordinated European plan of action. Where the argument becomes more confusing, but also more interesting, is whether either is more concerned with the policy or at what level it is implemented.

Such ideological arguments may seem absurd and irrelevant to those facing the reality of unemployment. Unfortunately, they are very real arguments that will have to be confronted at some point if policies are to emerge.

Not surprisingly, the majority of the Reflection Group, like the Commission, recommended European initiatives for the creation of jobs, and began the relevant part of their report by stressing "the urgent need to meet the challenge of job creation, in response to a pressing demand from Europe's citizens". Indeed, a majority saw further European integration as the key to job creation and favoured seeking coordinated European solutions, including:

- increased competitiveness,
- setting up a committee on employment to suggest policies and monitor the progress and the effect of other European Union policies on employment,
- investing in education, training and research, improving the Union's infrastructure and transport network through the structural funds (financial assistance that is channelled to the poorer regions of the Union – including parts of the UK),

- including a specific commitment to job creation in the treaty itself.

On the other hand, there will be those in the IGC who will argue that treaties do not help create employment. Their view will be that job creation comes from greater competitiveness, economic flexibility and reducing bureaucratic burdens and that it should remain a matter for member states in the light of individual circumstances.

Similar divisions are evident in discussions over the future of a European Social Dimension. Unfortunately, the social dimension is an area in which myths abound. A good example is the EU Directive which was reported, in some parts of the British media, as attempting to impose a 48 hour working week throughout the EU. In reality, the legislation, while providing for a maximum 48 hour week, made it clear that opt-outs were quite permissible if workers chose voluntarily to work for longer hours. In other words, the aim was to prevent the imposition of unacceptable working conditions, not to restrict those who choose freely to work for longer.

From the very beginning, the European Community has set standards for the provision of social welfare in both the public and private sectors of the economy. Its social legislation has extended the rights of the work-force to be consulted, to enjoy shorter working hours and it has also confirmed and extended the rights of working women, ethnic minorities and the disabled. Not surprisingly, the costs involved have been resented by some sectors of industry including some of Europe's major employers' confederations.

The UK Government, which has consistently opposed many of the provisions of the social dimension and opted out of the Social Chapter of the Maastricht Treaty, argues that these rights have increased labour costs in the European Union and have argued that they are making Europe uncompetitive in world markets. Increasingly these views are being echoed by some of the larger corporations on the continent, especially in Germany, where social costs are high. It is also true that some companies in the UK, where the social dimension is not enforcable, nevertheless operate many of its provisions. Ultimately, the member states of the European Union will have to decide whether they believe that social benefits need to be reduced in the face of cheaper labour costs in other parts of the world or whether prosperity will come from a highly skilled labour force with rights guaranteed within a social partnership. Although the former may be superficially attractive, it is likely that abandoning a social dimension would result in an immediate competitive downward spiral in workplace rights and provisions. At the same time, it is unlikely that the UK will be able to retain its 'opt-out' indefinitely because of the effect lower social costs has on the principle of the level playing field.

The environment

The environment has become a matter of enormous concern to most European citizens in a way that could not have been imagined when European integration was first discussed. Public opinion appears to be moving towards the idea of sustainable development, and this is being increasingly reflected in European legislation at all levels.

The questions and recommendations suggested by the Reflection Group include:

- the need to stress that the environment and sustainable development are priority objectives for the Union and that environmental considerations should always be considered alongside other policies, for example agriculture,

- the possibility of incorporating the decisions of the Rio Conference (a world-wide Environmental Conference held in Rio de Janeiro in 1994) into the treaty so that Community policies are geared to sustainable development,

- the need to ensure the full implementation of existing European environmental policies,

- the possibility of extending the use of qualified majority voting on environmental issues while bearing in mind the costs this could impose upon member states and the highly sensitive relationship of some environmental decisions (for example nuclear power) to issues of national sovereignty.

One member of the Reflection Group suggested that a commitment to phasing out nuclear energy entirely should be in the treaty, and was told that nuclear energy actually provided up to 75% of some member states' energy supply!

Transparency

There is a growing realisation throughout the Community's institutions that the need for citizens to be able to understand not only what emerges from the IGC but the whole bag of European treaties and legislation, must be urgently dealt with. This can be summed up in the simple question: how can citizens be better informed?

The IGC will thus consider whether:

* access to information might be a part of the treaty or be developed through a Commission and Council Code of Conduct (in other words, should freedom of access to information to be guaranteed by law or left in the hands of politicians and civil servants?)
* studies leading up to Commission proposals should be made public and greater advance notice given to national parliaments, including the production of Green papers for discussion,
* Union law, including the treaties, should be made clearer and simpler,
* the 1996 conference should result in a simpler treaty,
* the full Treaty on European Union might be simplified, taking out obsolete provisions, simplifying the language and making it more accessible to non-specialists.

Subsidiarity

Having been introduced in the Maastricht Treaty, it was clear that one subject ready for review would be subsidiarity. In dealing with this thorny subject, the Reflection Group made the interesting observation that "subsidiarity imposed not just a legal but also a behavioural obligation". In other words, subsidiarity is as much about the spirit as the letter of the law. The problem is that, on the one hand, there is too much lip-service and not enough practical action to ensure that decisions are taken at the right level, and, on the other, subsidiarity can be used as an excuse to 're-nationalise' powers that had previously been allocated at the European level.

Unfortunately, the issue of 'subsidiarity' goes to the heart of the concept of sovereignty, and it is exceptionally difficult to persuade national politicians about the 'spirit' of the Treaty. One suggestion is that there should be more effective contol over the application of subsidiarity both by the Commission and the Court of Justice, a suggestion likely to be opposed by precisely those national politicians who interpret subsidiarity as a struggle to repatriate as many powers as possible. Another, is that a special chamber consisting of national parliamentarians should be charged with establishing whether or not European legislation conforms to the principles of subsidiarity.

Other practical suggestions have been raised:

- one way of ensuring that member states' views on subsidiarity are taken into account without leaving it all in the hands of governments could be to establish a High Level Advisory Committee, consisting of two members from each national parliament, who could report on whether subsidiarity had been properly observed,

- that the Committee of the Regions be involved in deciding questions of subsidiarity. (This was a suggestion made by the Committee of the Regions but rejected by the Reflection Group who argued that it was not up to that Committee to interpret the application of the principle of subsidiarity between the Union and the member states.)

- that there be a principle which ensures that Community decisions do not put intolerable financial burdens on member states' budgets. There must be a consistency between the Union's ambitious proposals and the constraints upon the member states' budgets.

Subsidiarity, of course, works both ways in that some decisions presently at a lower level might benefit from decision-making at a higher level. In this context, the case was put, though not universally accepted, for more Community involvement in areas such as health, education, training and social policy.

Once more, this is potentially a major area of controversy as it deals with the critical question of who has power over what. Because all parties involved are nervous about reopening previous agreements, it is unlikely that the IGC will try to redefine the powers and competences of the Union, because it might mean a major treaty revision. On the other hand, is tinkering with the edges sufficient for a long term solution?

14. The budget

With the possible exception of regulations concerning the shape of bananas or cucumbers, nothing arouses as much passion as how the European Union spends its money. Not surprisingly, most people are concerned as to how their money is being spent and, as with most European issues, the facts are rarely explained in the press or other media.

The European Commission prepares the first draft of the budget. The draft is then passed to the EP whose members will have a vast number of projects – some of their own design and many submitted by interest groups – that they wish to see financed. Clearly not all new projects will survive and there will be much bargaining and compromise as they pass through various committees. Finally, the budget requires the approval of the Council of Ministers which, being more directly concerned with the revenue implications for the member states, tends to apply the brake to spending.

The total budget for the European Union has risen from 1.7% of the member states' total expenditure at the beginning of the 1980s to 2.4% in 1995. At 76 billion ECUs, it represents about 1.24% of the fifteen member states' total gross domestic product.

So how is it spent? Only about 5% of the budget goes on administration, much of which is swallowed up in the need to work in all the official languages. Quite clearly, it is necessary for all those taking part in debates and making decisions to have relevant information in their own language. This cost will increase considerably if further Union enlargement brings a further dozen or so official langauges each of which will need translation into all the others.

External action, including the European Union's commitment to Third World development accounts for approximately 5 billion ECUs. The fifteen member states of the European Union are not only the Third World's chief trading partner but are now the world's leading provider of public development aid.

The Common Agricultural Policy

By far the largest part of the European Union's budget, nearly 50% is committed to the Common Agricultual Policy (CAP). The objectives of the Common Agricultural Policy were set by the treaties at a time when Europe was still concerned with the need to ensure adequate food production and a fair standard of living for the agricultural community.

Specifically, the Common Agricultural Policy had four objectives:

* to increase agricultural productivity,
* to stabilise markets,
* to guarantee security of supply, and
* to ensure reasonable prices for consumers.

For Britain, joining the European Community late meant not being able to influence the discussions which led to the creation of the Common Agricultural Policy. With an exceptionally efficient agricultural sector and a historical trade in agricultural goods with other parts of the world, especially the Commonwealth, common market membership increased the price of some foods in Britain. This was offset against the commercial advantages of being able to trade freely within the European Community.

The system of subsidy, however, which led to gross over-production in the mid-1980s – the so-called wine lakes and cereal mountains – was substantially reformed by the Council of Ministers in 1992.

It may be that with climatic changes leading to increased concern about food production world-wide, the pendulum will swing, once more, towards a need to guarantee food supply. Nevertheless, it is quite clear that further reform of the CAP will be required if there is to be any chance of enlarging the Union to include the new democracies of Central and Eastern Europe. The accession of just Poland, the Czech Republic, Slovenia and Hungary would substantially increase the cost of the Common Agricultural Policy as it now stands. Not only has the CAP proved costly to the tax-payer but it has failed to take sufficient account of changing environmental standards or the needs of developing nations.

Although it will not be formally discussed within the IGC, the future of the Common Agricultural Policy will be raised when the whole question of the budget is up for review in 1998.

One related issue, which is causing increased concern in the UK, may be raised, however. The question of the transportation of livestock is causing a number of animal welfare groups to lobby for a treaty change in the definition of livestock from 'agricultural produce' to 'sentient beings'. As with environmental issues including the growing demand for organic produce, the treatment and transport of livestock opens wider issues than can be contained simply within the CAP.

The Regional and Social funds

'Cohesion' is the term used to describe the support system – the Structural (Regional and Social) funds – created to enable resources to be allocated to projects in the poorer regions of the European Union. They are directed at reducing the disparities of wealth between regions in the European Union and in improving the employment situation. As with the vast bulk of the Union's budget, the revenue is redistributed within the member states. Essentially, the funds represent investment designed to strengthen the European Union's economic potential and would have to be borne in any case by the member states if the Union did not exist. Presently, the Regional and Social Funds account for approximately 30% of the Union's total financial commitments but, as with the CAP, they would have to rise substantially with further enlargement. Not surprisingly, those regions, largely in the peripheral areas of the European Union and most particularly, the southern Mediterranean countries, are concerned that the enlargement should not mean loss of existing regional and social support.

Most countries have benefited by receiving payments from the Structural Funds set up to support infrastructure spending and education and training. The kind of projects that have been financed by these funds include building road and rail links, assisting enterprise centres and supporting exhibition centres such as the one in Birmingham. The funds are spent on key policies designed to increase employment opportunities – education and training – developing infrastructure services, including transport and health facilities, and encouraging private investment. Grants are almost invariably subject to matching funds being awarded by national governments, and are not designed to replace existing governmental expenditure. It was estimated that between 1989 and 1993, the European Structural Funds helped to provide 500,000 new jobs.

An increasing number of British local authorities have applied for and received funding under the Structural Funds. EU funds are also allocated for research and development, particularly in scientific and technological fields which are considered as vital to ensuring Europe's economic success in the future. Over 3½% of the European Union's total financial commitments are allocated to research teams working on a wide variety of technological and health issues including cancer and AIDS research.

Unsurprisingly, financing the Union has always been a vexed issue. Net contributors, those countries which pay more into the Community than they receive in financial benefits, have seen this as an acceptable price to pay to gain access to the wider markets of the European Union. Although this will continue to make good economic sense, with growing unemployment and soaring social costs in even the richest member states, the size and scope of the Union's budget will be more closely examined than before. As Britain's gross domestic product has declined in comparison with its European Union partners, however, it has received a proportionally greater share of the Structural Funds.

Although a full review of the way the European Union raises and spends money is not due until the end of the century, the IGC will need to examine very carefully the budgetary implications of any decisions it might make. This is an extremely difficult task further complicated by the uncertain cost of enlargement not just for the Union as a whole but also for the institutions.

There is also a determination to boost the fight against fraud which, though less extensive than is often presumed, nevertheless is a drain on the Union's resources. Although it is one of the pre-eminent arguments used against the European Union as a whole, all the evidence suggests that the finger of blame points mainly at the failure of the member states' governments to take sufficiently stringent action. Nevertheless, tightening the rules and strengthening cooperation procedures will be one of the tasks facing the IGC.

15. Economic and monetary union

The chances of the European Union moving towards a single currency in the next few years is undoubtedly having an enormous influence upon the course of the IGC even though it is not officially on the IGC's agenda. Conversely, getting the mood and the timing right will almost certainly be affected by the results of the IGC.

If the date for the introduction of a single currency is delayed or even abandoned, an important message will have been sent to both Europe's leaders and its citizens. At its most positive, it will provoke speedy and comprehensive action to consolidate and reinforce what has already been achieved. At worst, it will signal the unravelling of some of the most cherished hopes and dreams of the past fifty years. On the other hand, it is possible that pressing ahead could have exactly the same effect. If the timetable is too rigid and does not take into account sufficiently the different economic and political circumstances of the member states, it could provoke widespread discontent that could also damage the cohesion of the Union.

Like many European issues, although its details are extremely complicated, the broad concept of economic and monetary union is straightforward.

It is all about whether we should have a single currency that can be used throughout Europe or the 14 currencies we have now with the prospect of several more as new countries join the Union.

Three questions arise immediately:

- why have a single currency?
- is it a good idea?
- will it happen?

If Europe is to unite and build a single market, it is doubtful whether this could be properly achieved without a single currency. It would be hard to imagine a thriving economy in a country divided into several currency areas. For example, it is unlikely that the United States of America would have achieved its pre-eminent world economic position if it had continued with separate currencies in its fifty states. While the European Union is not a country but a union of member states, in economic terms the same reasoning can be applied.

A single currency unifies the payment system in a domestic market. It creates one market for savings and credit, for stocks and bonds, for pension funds and mortgages. It eliminates the cost of changing money. No more queuing at the Bureau de Change when you go on holiday – the first cup of coffee on the continent can be bought with the same notes and coins as the last cup of tea in Britain. It takes one important risk out of investment. For example, at present if you are thinking of building a factory in Yorkshire, you have no currency exposure but if you are thinking about building a factory or buying a retirement home in Spain, you have to worry about the future value of the Spanish peseta against the pound.

If there is to be a genuinely single market in Europe, therefore, it seems likely that a single currency will come in due course. If it does not, there is nothing to stop individual countries devaluing their own currencies and making their goods cheaper for sale elsewhere in the Union. This amounts to unfair competition and might eventually lead to the break up of the single market.

The Exchange Rate Mechanism, or ERM, which the UK and Italy ignominiously left in 1992, was an attempt to bring the European economies closer together by applying strict disciplines on governments to eliminate competitive devaluations and to encourage convergence in preparation for a single currency.

As it happens, the disciplines proved too strict. External events, particularly a recession in the United States and the stresses and strains in Germany following reunification and the linking of the East and West German currencies on a one-for-one basis, stretched the Exchange Rate Mechanism to breaking point.

This experience underlines the fact that however desirable a single currency may be in theory, it is extremely important – if it is to be a success – for the countries involved to be at approximately the same point in the economic cycle and to be broadly similar in their standards of living and rates of growth, inflation and unemployment.

The Maastricht Treaty, which provided the blueprint for the new single currency, laid down four 'convergence criteria' which each country that aspires to sign up to the single currency must adhere to. These criteria were designed to ensure that countries joining the new single currency area would not be too out of line economically and thus a threat to themselves and the system. The four criteria are:

- price stability: a rate of inflation no more than 1½% above the average of the three best performing members states,

- interest rates no more than 2 percentage points above the average of the three best performing states over the previous twelve months,

- no excessive government deficit i.e. not above 3% of Gross Domestic Product (GDP); public debt should not exceed 60% of GDP,

- exchange rate fluctuations in the European Monetary System should not exceed their normal margins for at least two years.

At the time of writing, only Luxembourg actually meets all four criteria. Britain is fairly well placed, but France is having to apply draconian measures to control its budget deficit and even Germany failed the public deficit test last year and looks like doing the same in 1996.

It may not be possible to answer objectively the question of whether Europe should press ahead with a single currency – it depends on what you believe and what you want. There are clearly advantages and disadvantages and it should be up to all those who will be affected to form a judgment. For those who believe in the overall objective of European unity whether for purely practical or idealistic reasons, economic and monetary union is an essential building block for union.

On the other hand, for those who believe that as much power as possible should be kept in the hands of national governments, then monetary union, by definition, is a bad thing. Between these two poles there is not much room for compromise. No doubt domestic concerns will affect the readiness of individual states to enter into a single currency. What is important, however, is to try and untangle some of the economic arguments from the political ones.

Part of the confusion is that both sides have a tendency to use both political and economic arguments without making clear the difference. For example, the 'founding fathers' of Europe saw economic and monetary union not merely as an economic tool for prosperity but as one of the most powerful binding agents between countries. If their final objective was perpetual peace in Europe and the means to get there was economic integration, then a single currency would be a fundamental step forward in that process. This approach has also underlined the thinking of many pro-Europeans since then. Apart from their politcal belief in a single currency, they are also persuaded that there is a sound economic case for a single currency.

On the other side, many of those who argue against economic and monetary union as either unworkable or economically harmful are, in fact, primarily defending their belief in the ultimate sovereignty of the nation state. For example, to counter the argument for a single currency by arguing that it removes many of the Chancellor of the Exchequer's powers of manoeuvre is as much a political as an economic argument.

The British government's judgement about the British economy may be much better than anything that could be reached at the European level. However, its prime concern may not be the long term future of the British economy but ensuring its party wins the next election.

It may be that the British, or any other European people, will prefer to keep their system as it is, despite the possibility of government manipulation of the economy for electoral reasons because they place their trust in the accountability of governments to their national parliaments and parliaments to their electorates. Or it may be that they would feel safer if at least some key factors, like the value of the currency, were guaranteed by an independent authority.

In other words, the economic case for economic and monetary union, if it can be proved, may not necessarily be enough by itself to convince voters to change their support for the *status quo*. Equally, those who are undecided should beware of the political ideologies that often lie hidden behind apparently economic arguments. Ultimately, the argument rests on a mixture of values and self-interest.

For example, why has France long made sharing monetary decision-making with the powerful German Bundesbank central to its European objectives? One reason is entirely pragmatic: like it or not, the power of the Deutschmark and the Bundesbank is a reality and cannot be wished away. Successive French governments have seen it in their interest to move towards a system in which German and other member states' influence on the control of French money would be more than compensated by French and others' influence over German money. In other words, pooling monetary sovereignty, in this case, is perceived as beneficial for all concerned as well as contributing to a more stable and secure Europe.

The political argument is as much domestic as European. Can politicians resist the temptation to print money and inflate the economy in the run-up to elections? Is it better that the creation and control of money should be entrusted to an independent Central Bank free of government interference and responsible constitutionally to maintain the value of money whatever government is in power? The Bank of England was nationalised in 1946 and, since then, the pound has lost about 90% of its value. The Bundesbank in Germany is independent of government and has earned the respect of the German people by maintaining the value of the Deutschmark for half a century.

The proposed European Central Bank, the constitution of which was set out in the Maastricht Treaty, has been modelled on the German Bundesbank.

Recently, it has become fashionable to make central banks more independent. The Banque de France has been divorced from government and even the Bank of England has been given back a degree of independence, with the monthly meetings of the Governor of the Bank and the Chancellor of the Exchequer being opened up to public scrutiny by the publication of their discussions albeit four weeks after the event.

Up to now, we are talking politics. What about the economic pros and cons of the single currency?

The most obvious advantage of a single currency in Europe is that the same notes and coins would be used throughout the European Union, and the cost and bother of changing from one money to another would be eliminated.

But much more importantly, it would create a single capital market of 350 million people initially (assuming that all member states were to join) rising perhaps to 500 million with the addition of new members. This would be the largest capital market in the world. The savings of German farmers, for instance, would be available to finance job creation in the wider European Community. This vast capital market could supply the depth and liquidity for productive investment on the scale required to compete in the global economy of the next century. In other words, it would help minimise the cost of capital for industry.

Companies would no longer have to worry about exchange rates when exporting or importing from other European Union countries. This should particularly help smaller companies expand their businesses. Setting up a factory in another country, for example, would be less risky. Prices could be directly compared with prices at home and the same bank and insurance company could help with the transaction.

The new European currency would become a major world trading and reserve currency, matching the dollar and the yen. Denominating world trade in your own currency further reduces risk. When other nations hold your currency for trading purposes or as a reserve (spare cash) it represents a loan – that is to say another source of capital – which helps to keep the cost of borrowing and investment as low as possible.

A single currency means a single balance of payments between Europe and the rest of the world. At the moment, over 40% of Britain's economy is foreign trade. We are highly exposed to what is going on in the rest of the world. External events have a major impact on our economy, and can cause major fluctuations and volatility. With a single currency, much of what is now external trade would be classed as internal and our exposure to external trade risks would drop to about 15% – closer to the levels existing in the US and Japan. This should further reduce uncertainty and volatility, again promoting lower levels of interest rates and stability.

All of these developments would also benefit the City of London and Britain's financial services industry, which is one of the largest and most efficient in the world. They would encourage an inflow of foreign investment which in turn would help to create jobs.

What then are the arguments against a single currency? Primarily they are about the loss of economic freedom and flexibility. We would no longer, for example, be free to devalue our currency in times of crisis.

One objection arises in the case where the economies of participating countries prove to be too divergent, internal pressures may build up, which could give rise to regional imbalances and a need for prosperous areas to prop up less prosperous areas. Would taxpayers in one country be prepared to finance the shortfalls in another?

It is also argued that the social costs of employment – social security, sickness benefit, holidays, maternity leave and particularly pensions – are much higher in continental countries than they are in Britain. Adopting a single currency might force us to adopt higher prices, making us less competitive in world markets and leading to job losses. With Britain having the highest level of private pensions throughout Europe, will British taxpayers find themselves having to help subsidise other member states' public pension funds as Europe's population grows older?

There will be costs involved in the change over from one currency to another. Not only will shopkeepers, and others, need to become familiar with the new currency but some equipment, like coin-operated machines, will have to be changed to accept new notes and coins.

There is also a concern that financial or fiscal irresponsibility on the part of the government of one or more member states might adversely affect the interests of more responsible member states.

Will a single currency reduce the UK's flexibility to concentrate more on world markets, particularly in Asia where growth is likely to be most dynamic in the next century? Or would a strong European market serve as a springboard for developing trade world-wide?

Being outside the single currency would not necessarily damage the City of London. The main market for the new currency might well remain in London, just as we now make markets in dollars, yen and other currencies and financial assets. Nor would investment from abroad necessarily be discouraged – indeed, it might be encouraged by lower labour costs as part of a more flexible approach. But would this be worth the risk of possibly having to pay higher rates of interest than our neighbours, and the risk of retaliation from our partners in the European Union if we were seen to be lowering the value of the pound in order to gain competitive advantage for our exports in the context of the single market?

As will be quite obvious, many of the arguments on both sides are unquantifiable. Indeed, many respected business people and commentators believe that the balance of advantage and disadvantage, at least in the short run, is close. Furthermore there are some important issues which do not strictly fall on one side of the argument or other but pose serious problems that will need to be resolved.

Most important of these is the question of the European Central Bank's accountability. That it must be accountable is not in dispute, what is less clear is to whom the Bank should be made accountable. In principle, it will be independent in its actions, not taking instructions from anyone, whether EC institutions, governments or anyone else. In practice, it will have to answer to all the European Union's main institutions if it fails to fulfil its central obligations.

For some people, this provides a guarantee that the Bank will be free of political interference; for others it is unacceptable that a body whose decisions will have such an important effect on key issues such as taxation and employment throughout the European Union should be unaccountable to an elected body.

As with so many of the problems outlined, attitudes towards the Central Bank depend on political values. A further problem arises: to whom should the Bank be accountable? If to the Council of Ministers, then every meeting may be a political squabble. If to the EP, it might be used for political ends. Is there a difference between political responsibility and accountability? The Bundesbank and the US Federal Reserve are accountable for meeting their criteria and have the executive power to achieve their targets. These uncertainties might be used by some as an argument against joining. But they can equally be seen as part of a broader pan-European debate not about whether economic and monetary union should happen but about what it should look like.

There are many other problems to be resolved before any final decision can be taken. For example, how will transfer payments between countries be resolved. Will richer countries have to subsidise the welfare systems of the poorer nations and regions and, therefore, pay higher taxes than would have been the case otherwise? The UK has greater owner occupation than the rest of Europe – what might this mean for interest rates? If European interest rates go up, the effect on British mortgage holders will be far greater than on rent payers on the continent. What about total taxation? With the demography of Europe changing, the UK will have a higher proportion of taxable citizens in twenty years than other parts of Europe. Will we have to shoulder a greater part of the taxation burden? All these important day-to-day issues will need to be resolved before a final decision can be taken.

There is one further suggestion that has been aired, particularly in the UK, without finding much support among other member states but which might yet play a part in moves towards a single currency: could the 'Euro' be introduced as an alternative currency that could be used alongside national currencies throughout the European Union, rather than as a single currency? This would certainly be possible and it has been argued that it would be a 'market choice' solution to a single currency. If people liked it and wanted it, it would eventually take over from national currencies. If it was rejected, then its unpopularity would be self-evident.

It would have the advantage of introducing choice and allowing for greater flexibility in the convergence criteria but one of its disadvantages would be the confusion caused to businesses and consumers alike trying to cope with two currencies and dealing with the transaction costs involved.

Like all great leaps forward in the movement towards European integration, economic and monetary union will come about through a combination of member states' political will and their economic ability to deliver. Although, at the moment, there is considerable uncertainty on both fronts, the project is still likely to succeed.

It is clear that the convergence criteria make good sense. If all the member states are to live together in one financial house, then it is important that no one state incurs debts and liabilities that will become the responsibility of all the rest. Once exchange rates have been fixed, governments can no longer use potentially inflationary measures, like issuing currency, to solve short term liquidity problems, nor can they devalue their currencies in order to boost competitiveness as a way to reduce unemployment. Once a single currency is in use, the real power of national governments to use currency to alter its economic strategy will be lost forever. On the other hand, the convergence criteria and a single currency will introduce a new and long-term sense of responsibility to governments that have been able to resort to short-term measures to boost their electoral chances.

The real problem, however, has not been in recognising the value of the convergence criteria but in trying to apply them. The discipline involved is hard enough for governments used to manipulating interest and exchange rates as well as borrowing in order to achieve their political and economic objectives. But it also comes at a time when Europe has found it extremely difficult to lift itself out of recession.

In France, although the attempt to cut back spending led to riots in the streets it seems increasingly likely that President Chirac will succeed in his efforts to implement the convergence criteria. In Italy and Belgium, which have high levels of debt, and Spain, where unemployment is over twenty percent, however, the pain could be even greater.

A BRILLIANT CONSPIRACY?

There is a fear that the convergence criteria, which are designed to be anti-inflationary, may turn out to be so deflationary that they will defeat, at least in the short run, Europe's chances of long-term economic recovery. On the other hand, it may be that, in the long run, Europe's best hope of long-term prosperity rests with the advantages that a single, stable currency will add to the single market.

The political will to move towards economic and monetary union remains extremely strong in the French, German and Benelux governments and any failure to implement the Maastricht Treaty in full and may result in their going forward alone.

Of course, if the present moves towards economic and monetary union falter, it does not mean that they will not be revived later. Nor does it preclude the possibility that, in a single market, with no exchange rates, one individual currency might become so favoured as to become, in effect, a single currency.

None of these is impossible, but perhaps the final point should be taken from the report of the German Constitutional Court which, having approved the Maastricht Treaty, albeit with a certain reluctance, stated that any further moves towards economic and monetary union would have to be accompanied by a serious attempt to reform and democratise the Union's institutions – the task of the next IGC. It is the linking of the introduction of a single currency to the strengthening of the democratic process that distinguishes the federalist approach to economic and monetary union. Indeed, it is the only approach that meets at least some of the objections of the most thoughtful and rigorous economic critics of monetary union.

The European Currency Unit or ECU was originally intended to be the single currecny for Europe. The ECU was the central feature of the European Monetary System (EMS) established in 1978. The EMS defined the ECU as a basket of the member states' currencies. The weighting of each currency within the basket was determined by the size of the respective economies and initially was revised every five years. Germany had the largest weighting of over 30%. The EMS also laid down a mechanism for keeping member states' exchange rate fluctuations within defined bands. This was intended to encourage convergence by forcing governments to adopt policies that maintained a stable value for their currencies. This mechanism was called the Exchange Rate Mechanism (ERM).

There were several adjustments to exchange rates within the system in the early years but in the early 1990s the pressure built up to explosive levels. The reasons for this are complex but a major contributing factor was the unexpected re-unification of Germany and the economic consequences of uniting the East and West German currencies on a one-to-one basis. A further pressure on the EMS came when referenda in Denmark and France threatened to prevent the ratification of the Maastricht Treaty and therefore the introduction of a single currency within a set timetable. The ERM effectively collapsed in September 1992 when Britain and Italy left the system on 'Black Wednesday'. Further upheavals took place in 1993, leading to a widening of the bands of fluctuation.

The break up of the ERM caused the devaluation of the ECU basket. This discrediting of the ECU was a major reason for changing the name of the proposed single currency to the 'Euro'.

Under the Maastricht Treaty and subsequent decisions at the Madrid summit in December 1995, the programme for the introduction of the single currency is as follows:

Early 1998

The political decision will be made on which member states meet the convergence criteria and will adopt the single currency.

1st January 1999

Exchange rates between the participating member states will be irrevocably fixed and the basket will cease to exist. The value of the new Euro will be fixed in terms of the currencies of the participating member states and the Euro will become an internationally traded currency. The new European Central Bank will come into being, its forerunner – the European Monetary Institute – will cease to exist. All wholesale monetary operations in the foreign exchange market will be conducted in Euros. BUT, national notes and coins will continue to exist and most retail transactions including shopping and banking will continue to use national currencies. Dual pricing in shops will become increasingly common.

2002 approximately

New notes and coins in the Euro denomination will be introduced and national notes and coins withdrawn. The new notes and coins may have familiar national symbols on one side and a common European design on the reverse.

16. The Eastern dimension

Although representatives from some Central and Eastern European countries attended the original Congress of Europe at the Hague in 1948, any suggestion that they could share in the integration of Europe vanished with the construction of the Iron Curtain. For the next forty years or so, it was exclusively a project for Western Europe. In 1989, however, as the 'velvet' revolutions, which started in Czechoslovakia (now the Czech and Slovak Republics), Hungary, East Germany and Poland, spread to Romania, Bulgaria, Albania and the republics of the former Soviet Union, it became immediately clear that European integration could not and should not be restricted to the West.

That such momentous and optimistic events should generate high expectations was not surprising although they were soon replaced by a more sober sense of reality. Nevertheless, it remained clear that the eventual accession of the democracies of Central and Eastern Europe was of fundamental importance not simply for moral reasons but in order to guarantee European peace and stability.

At a number of European Council summit meetings, most particularly that in Copenhagen in 1993, firm commitments were made to bring the countries of Central and Eastern Europe – in particular Poland, Hungary and the Czech and Slovak Republics – into the European Union as swiftly as possible. East Germany, of course, had already acceded as a result of reunification with the Federal Republic of Germany.

The political commitment notwithstanding, the real economic and political hurdles that will need to be overcome before the accession of these new members is formidable.

The last round of enlargement, which brought Austria, Finland and Sweden into the Union at the beginning of 1995, was greatly simplified by the fact that the standard of living in the applicant countries was above the average of the Union as a whole. Not only did they have existing and important trading relations with the member states of the Union, but many of the economic obstacles to trade had already been removed when the European Free Trade Association, to which they belonged, negotiated a free trade area with the European Union.

At the same time, the three entrants had traditions of stable, democratic government and, in the case of Sweden, higher standards of open government than has yet been dreamt of by most of the member states of the European Union.

Such advantages, however, do not yet apply to the countries of Eastern and Central Europe. Nor are they the first in the queue – applications had already been received from Cyprus, Malta and Turkey and, while a substantial question mark hangs over Turkey on a number of issues, including human rights, trade agreements are in place for Cyprus and Malta, in advance of proper negotiations for entry.

Nevertheless, wide ranging association agreements, generally known as 'Europe Agreements' have been concluded with six Central and East European states: Bulgaria, the Czech Republic, Hungary, Poland, Romania, and the Slovak Republic and it is expected that similar agreements will soon be concluded with Slovenia and the three Baltic Republics and in the longer term also with Albania and Croatia.

Provisions of the agreements include:

- the progressive introduction of free trade in industrial goods over a ten year period,
- the removal by the EU of tariffs and other trade barriers at a faster rate than will be carried out by the applicant countries with some special exceptions,
- the need for the associated states to ensure that their laws in relation to the operation of their economies are brought into line with EU law, for example with respect to state aids, competition, banking, insurance etc.,
- and that special joint councils and committees are set up to bring about a political dialogue on a wide range of issues of mutual interest.

Practical issues are rarely dealt with in formal agreements. To bring their economies to a level at which entry into the Union is possible, the applicant countries need trade and investment. Unfortunately, their attempts to increase exports to the European Union are often frustrated by the Common Agricultural Policy, which protects the European Union's farmers from competition, and by the accusation of 'dumping' made by threatened western companies.

There is also a real fear that the cost of enlargement will prove prohibitive. As well as the potential cost to the cohesion funds, an impossible strain would also be placed on the Common Agricultural Policy support system if it were to continue on its present basis. An alternative, of course, might be the thorough-going reform of the CAP that has been long overdue. But this would have enormous political implications for those countries with large farming lobbies.

As already noted, the southern Mediterranean countries are concerned that the cost of enlargement should not reduce the support that they currently receive from the structural funds.

On the other hand, the price of the failure to embrace the new European democracies and integrate them swiftly into the Union might, in the long run, prove even more costly. The cost of maintaining peace is far lower than the potential cost of returning to a divided and unstable continent. And, while emphasis is being placed on the applicant states' ability to demonstrate that their democratic reform programmes have taken root and are now irreversible, this could be meaningless unless there is a firm commitment to welcoming the applicant countries into the Union.

For the time being, however, work is being undertaken to assist in the "progressive integration of the political and economic systems, as well as the foreign and security policies of the associated states and the Union, together with increasing cooperation in the fields of justice and home affairs, so as to create an increasingly unified area". In order to further this process, the heads of state and prime ministers of the Visegrad countries have been invited to participate in European Council meetings and there is growing contact with both the EP and the Council of Ministers.

17. Time for a constitution

If, despite every attempt to keep them simple, the preceding chapters give the impression that the EU is all something of a muddle, that's because it is. The advantages that came from the European Union growing *sui generis* into a system of supra-national government are fast being overtaken by the confusion arising from its complexity and the growing gap of understanding between the "Keepers of the Mystery" and the general public. Unless this gap is closed swiftly, there is a real possibility that the whole process could fall apart.

Ian Davidson made the point in *The Independent* two years ago:

> If the IGC fails, it is not absolutely improbable that the European Union could break up. What is much more likely is that it will disintegrate into different layers of membership in which Germany, together with France and the Benelux (and perhaps others) would press ahead to create an inner political and economic core. That is the kind of power struggle – in which different member states vote with their feet – that may lie at the end of the IGC of 1996.

This may well be welcomed by the so-called 'Eurosceptics'. Some of them have already called for a renegotiation of the Treaty of Rome in order to turn the European Union into a free trade area managed on an inter-governmental basis: in other words a single market without a political dimension.

As has been fully discussed, the subsequent lack of accountability implicit in inter-governmental decision-making would amount to removing the ability of European citizens to control decision-making at the European level and create in Stephen Woodard's shrewdly perceptive phrase a 'ministocracy'. Far from citizens having a greater control over European decision-making, it would become even more a mystery understood only by an elite.

But there is an equally fundamental reason why the dismantling of the existing institutions would be profoundly mistaken: it would remove the glue which binds the member states together in times of uncertainty or disagreement. Supporters of European integration have become used to being called unrealistic for believing in the power of the European idea to bind the peoples of Europe together. In reality such an aspiration is infinitely more realistic than a belief that the single market alone would create the conditions necessary for the preservation of long term peace and stability. Indeed, it may have exactly the opposite effect if a conflict of interest arises between member states.

It is only too easy to conceive of circumstances in which a failure to secure national interests, stirred by the media, could lead to the re-emergence of trade barriers and a breakdown of normal relations between states. Without international institutions that can claim a popular democratic legitimacy, inter-governmentalism would be too frail to withstand many of the pressures of domestic politics and national ambitions.

There have always been politicians whose certainty in their own values, ideology and powers of persuasion has deluded them into believing that they can obtain lasting advantage for their countries through a mixture of force and diplomacy. Gratifying though this may be to their egos, the results are rarely of benefit to ordinary people. The result of the dazzling and complex diplomatic manoeuvring of the nineteenth century was not a balance of advantage for the people of Europe, but the unparalleled devastation of the First World War.

What is extraordinary is how quickly the memory of such momentous failure seems to fade. One of the central ideas underlying the post-war European construction was to minimise the destructive potential of political ego-maniacs, which is presumably why so many of them are implacably opposed to it. With all its faults, the European Union is predicated on the idea that the solution to inter-state disputes should be sought in rational discussion. Of course, every member state seeks to maximise its own interests, but the institutions were devised to promote co-operation rather than conflict; consensus above division; the common cause rather than mere self-interest.

It is precisely because they understand extremely clearly the dangers of unfettered nationalism that post-war German governments have clung so firmly to the European ideal. Yet the prejudice lingers on that the European Union is yet another attempt by Germany to impose its national interests on its neighbours; that having been defeated in war twice this century it believes it can impose its will through the medium of the Union. Such attitudes run surprisingly deep in the British psyche and help explain the widespread misunderstanding of Chancellor Kohl's recently stated worries that a failure to bring about full European economic, monetary and political union could leave Europe vulnerable to war again in the future. The point he was making, and which had been made by previous German Chancellors including Helmut Schmidt in his Dimbleby lecture, was that it is precisely because Germany has been a threat to the security of Europe and needs to be contained within legally binding and enforceable structures, that European Union is so vital. The key to post-war German politics has been the willingness to subordinate German self-interest into the broader interests of Europe – the building of a European Germany not a German Europe. Kohl's warning, which will be ignored at our peril, is that we must understand that neither historical guilt nor the opportunity to bind German interests into the wider interests of Europe will last forever.

It is the same point made by Neal Ascherson in a recent article in *The Independent on Sunday*:

> Ten days ago, the Prime Minister of Bavaria broke a taboo – the holiest in German politics. Edmund Stoiber proclaimed that the time had come to put the interests of the German nation-state first and to halt the growth of 'an overshadowing, undermining European federal state.' When Hans-Dietrich Genscher was foreign minister, he used to say that 'the more European our foreign policy is, the more national it is ... ' If Germany gives up on European union, all certainties collapse under us like a rotten floor and we plunge down into darkness. Down there, nation states strike out blindly at one another. Integration gives way to bilat-

eral alliances as European states seek allies against their neighbours. Germany, so reliable for half a century would become *unberechenbar* – unpredictable. At one moment, German national interests might dictate an alliance with France and Russia against Britain and Poland; at another, some Mitteleuropa between the Rhine, the Mediterranean and the Dnieper, designed to fortify a German-dominated central powerbloc. America would leave Europe to its own turmoil, while the free-trading core of the European idea would be poisoned by protectionism.

Perhaps more than anything else, it has been the failure to understand this fundamental issue, that has made Britain's role in Europe not merely ineffectual but at times deeply destructive. Margaret Thatcher's arrogant mistrust of the German post-war commitment to European Union had all the hallmarks of prejudice pretending to be insight.

Describing Lady Thatcher's views at a seminar she convened as Prime Minister, Professor Alan Watson argued:

She thus laid out her argument with brutal candour, or what Geoffrey Howe vividly describes as 'gut candour'. The Germans, because of their innate character defects and because of their very size and geographical position would always de-stabilise and pose a threat to their neighbours. That threat was no longer military but was now economic and political. The only way to contain it (the German drive to dominance), was through bilateral and trilateral alliances. Mrs Thatcher did not refer to the precursors of such alliances, namely those used to restrain and deter Wilhelmian Germany before the First World War. However, her instinct was clearly ... pre-First World War rather than post Second World War. Such alliances exemplify the traditional power diplomacy of the nineteenth century and, as she so accurately foresaw, are inconceivable in the European Union.

A BRILLIANT CONSPIRACY?

Which is precisely why the European Union, despite its many faults, continues to be such a vital construction not just for the present but for the future. In Zbiginiew Brezinski's words in his book *Out of Control*:

> The European Community is a miracle of the post war world. The bruises of Maastricht will take a while to heal, and doubtless there are useful lessons to be absorbed. How the Community now proceeds is for the members to decide but from the American vantage, the process of European integration, no matter how halting, is the long term foundation of European stability ... For Europe to play a more active world role, especially as America's co-equal, the decisive precondition is continued unification. Only a more united Europe – the very scale of which defines Europe as a genuine global power – is likely to infuse into the European outlook a more generous global vision. Short of that, Europe will run the risk of reverting to ancient feuds, of remaining selfishly absorbed by its internal problems, and of becoming preoccupied by its traditional concern with the power of Germany. That is why the promotion of a genuinely united Europe is in the fundamental interests of the world at large. Only such a Europe can undertake and is likely to assume the larger burdens of participation in the building of a global community based on the principle of freedom ...

That is the vision Europe should be aiming for, not a return to the insecurity and impotence of squabbling nation states. The whole point of the European Union is that the sharing of sovereignty applies to all the member states. It is self-evidently absurd to complain about the loss of British sovereignty without recognising that the same principles reduce the power of individual action for every other member state.

Underlying the success of the European Community, now the Union, for the past fifty years has been a belief that the advantages of accepting collective decisions underwritten by the rule of law outweighed the disadvantages, an idea expressed with great clarity by T. C. Hartley in *The Foundations of European Law*:

In contrast to past attempts, by Napoleon and Hitler for example, to unite Europe by force, the European Community is based on the consent of the member states. Underlying this consent is the tacit assumption that all the member states will play the game according to the same rules: national governments are prepared to accept rules of Community law which are against their interests but benefit others, if other member states are prepared to do the same when the balance of advantage is reversed. It follows from this that Community law must have the same meaning and effect in all member states: it would be wrong if Community law had greater effect in one country than in another.

But the acceptance of the rules by the member states may not necessarily be sufficient if the whole structure does not enjoy popular support. The key is the link between sovereignty and subsidiarity. Sovereignty has essentially two properties which have been integrated in the history and structure of the nation state. On the one hand, it refers to the highest expression of national or 'tribal' feelings, personified in the person of a 'sovereign' as in a constitutional monarchy or in the role of the presidency in a republic. On the other, it confers authority on a government and usually a parliament to make legislation and take executive decisions. In the nation state, these two attributes of sovereignty are combined. In other words, the government of a nation state exercises its authority with or without democratic support.

But this does not necessarily have to be the case. In a world of growing complexity and interdependence, it may be necessary to separate these two attributes of sovereignty. Those who argue that national feelings should not be suppressed are absolutely right; where this has happened, as events in the former Yugoslavia and the former Soviet Union illustrate, they will resurface with violent and unpredictable consequences. But that does not mean that there has to be an automatic link between national identity and every level of government.

There is no reason to believe that every decision must be taken at the national level for it to be popularly acceptable. NATO is built on the assumption that the defence of the western world required the sharing of sovereignty; environmental erosion cannot be contained within national borders; capital movements can severely reduce the power of a government to control its own economy; yet all of these activities carry broad (though not necessarily unanimous) public support. In Andrew Marr's words: "The erosion of national independence is a marginal subject, it seems, when we are talking about NATO, the bond market, real freedom to set corporate tax rates, or environmental standards. But it arouses hysterical passions when the European Union is at issue." If such passions are not openly confronted in the immediate future, they have the potential to weaken substantially if not destroy the movement towards European unity.

How can these passions be confronted? I believe there are three steps that must be taken: the first is to recognise that sovereignty should no longer be a property of the state but of individuals able to exercise it at the most appropriate level – the Jeffersonian principle that sovereignty belongs to the people who lend it to be exercised at different levels of government; the second is to incorporate this principle and the rights and responsibilities that flow from it into the framework of a European constitution; and the third is to submit such a constitution to the people of Europe for their approval or rejection.

The struggle between defenders of national sovereignty and promoters of multi-national institutions can only be resolved by agreeing decisions should be made by the most appropriate level of government acceptable to the majority of citizens. If this could be the guiding principle for the IGC, a clearer perspective would begin to emerge.

What is required is not another treaty amending previous treaties which are themselves couched in the obscure legislative jargon necessary to withstand challenges in an international court. Europe needs something far more fundamental if the aspirations of its people are to be met and their sense of alienation overcome. The danger with treaties is not that they create bad laws but that they can be seen as bad law. After World War One, there was a revulsion against duplicitous and secret bilateral diplomacy; today there is growing opposition to treaties that are cobbled together as a result of national horse-trading and compromise that effectively exclude amendments from any directly elected body.

As could be seen when Mrs Thatcher forced the Single European Act through parliament and Mr Major the Maastricht Treaty, the whole process is entirely unsatisfactory. While it was clear that a substantial majority of MPs from all parties supported the general principle of both treaties, not only were they unable to make any amendments, but the British parliamentary system made the issue appear more divisive than it really was.

The solution now has to be the creation of a constitution or, at the very minimum, a set of constitutional principles in which the aims, objectives, powers and competencies of the Union are clearly laid out in such a way that they can be understood by all European citizens, who should be able to approve or reject the proposals.

Ultimately, people are not moved by technicalities alone. They need vision to maintain the momentum when problems arise and frustrations appear to outweigh the immediate benefits. Treaties alone cannot inspire. Few people have read them and those who have will have been hard pressed to discover in their text any real sense of excitement or purpose.

As was made clear in chapter 2, federalism is not a way of creating a superstate by the back door, but a system of unifying free and equal peoples whose sovereignty is not diminished but extended and guaranteed by the rule of law. By appealing to a federal constitution, states can resist encroachment on their powers, individuals and local authorities can also appeal against arbitrary action by states. It is not even such an enormous step as it may appear. It is more about changing our way of looking at things than changing the way things really are.

Under a written constitution, we, as citizens, would have the right to demand openness and accountability from our governing institutions at every level. The responsibility would be ours for good or ill. In Andrew Marr's words:

> The more we are democratically involved, the more we are implicated, too: when mistakes do happen, as they must, we cannot simply blame them upon some anonymous or high-up body. Instead of seething and feeling

> put-upon, we take some responsibility and perhaps learn
> from them and so grow up a little. Being able to do this
> growing up is the difference between the political child-
> ishness of being a subject, slave or servant of the state
> and the condition of political adulthood, or citizenship.

What should a European constitution look like? Can the fundamental principles and structures presently contained in treaties running
to thousands of words be reduced to a simple and coherent document that could be understood by any literate person? I believe they
can. The American constitution is very short, yet has proved sufficiently resilient to survive for over two centuries.

A constitution for Europe is not a new idea. There have already
been numerous attempts at drafting such a document. The EP has
produced a number of working drafts, ranging from Altiero Spinelli's
Draft Treaty on European Union of 1984 to the most recent documents emerging from committees chaired by a former Spanish MEP,
now European Commissioner, Marcelino Oreja Aguirre, and the
Belgian MEP, Fernand Hermann.

I believe that a European constitution could be very simple and yet
remain effective. It should begin by stating the ultimate reasons for
the Union, which are the preservation of peace, the guarantee of
life, liberty and self-fulfilment for all citizens; the promotion of prosperity based on balanced and sustainable economic growth; the development of a legal and economic area without internal frontiers;
and the promotion of world order based on principles of justice,
fairness, democratic values and free trade.

Such a constitution would need to recognise that the allocation of
powers in the Union's institutions should be based upon two principles: the need to maintain a right and necessary balance between
the will of the citizens of Europe, as expressed through a directly
elected parliament on the one hand, and the authority of the governments and parliaments of the member states whose sovereign-
ties derive from distinct cultural, social and political traditions on
the other; and the devolution of power to the lowest level of government compatible with democratic principles, efficiency, the traditions of the member states and the preservation of the Union.

It should declare that the Union is composed of its citizens and its member states, that it can be joined by other democratic European states in the future and, most importantly, that member states would have the right to secede from the Union, acting under certain defined procedures.

The constitution should make it clear that, in those areas where the Union has competence, the Union's laws would take precedence over the law of the member states.

It should define the membership of the Union clearly, either by limiting it to those holding the nationality of a member state or by enlarging it to include certain defined residents from third countries. The rights of citizens to move and reside freely throughout the territory of the Union and enjoy the rights of citizenship of the member state in which they choose to live should be confirmed.

The constitution should confirm the Union's accession, as a whole, to the European Convention on Human Rights and Fundamental Freedoms and its applicability to all European citizens and other residents within the Union.

It should define the legislative, executive and judicial structures of the Union.

Co-decision on all legislative matters should be shared between the European Parliament representing the people of Europe directly and either the Council of Ministers representing the member states or, more democratically, an Assembly consisting of members of national parliaments.

The EP should be elected by direct universal suffrage for a five year period according to a uniform proportional electoral system, with the possibility of altering the number of MEPs and redrawing constituency boundaries by constitutional amendment.

The composition of the Council of Ministers (or an Assembly of national parliamentarians) should be left to the national governments or parliaments of the member states. In either case, however, voting should be in national groups by some form of qualified majority voting or double qualified majority voting (a majority of both states and their populations) according to the constitutional importance of the legislation.

A simple majority in the Parliament and a qualified majority in the Council (or the Assembly) should be required for the adoption of legislation; an absolute majority in the Parliament and a qualified majority in the Council (or Assembly) should be required for the adoption of the budget and for the censure of the Commission; and a two-thirds majority in the Parliament and a double qualified majority in the Council (or the Assembly) should be required to amend the constitution or enlarge the Union.

The European Commission should exercise executive authority on behalf of the Union in all matters within the Union's competence.

One Commissioner should be elected from each member state by the Parliament following nominations from the Council (or the Assembly). The Commission should be accountable both to the Parliament and to the Council or Assembly and may be dismissed collectively following a joint vote of censure.

The Commission should retain the power to initiate legislation, execute the budget and the laws of the Union, monitor compliance with the Constitution and other Union legislation and negotiate the Union's treaties with other countries.

The European Council should remain and would be composed of the Heads of State and Government of the member states and the Presidents of the Commission, the Parliament and (if it exists) the Assembly. It should be charged with reviewing the Union's legislative programme and setting the general political guidelines.

Voting in the European Council should be on a qualified majority basis as set down for the Council (or the Assembly).

But the European Council would also have the right to veto legislation adopted by the Parliament and the Council (or the Assembly) if it voted unanimously to do so.

The European Court of Justice should be deemed the Union's supreme judicial authority and should be empowered to interpret, and impose sanctions on those in violation of, the Constitution and the Union's treaties and legislation.

The Union should have a single currency with a European Central Bank authorised to control the supply of money but accountable to the EP and the Council (or the Assembly).

The Court of Auditors, the Economic and Social Committee and the Committee of the Regions should carry out the specific tasks provided for in the existing treaties.

The Union should have the power to make laws appertaining directly to the benefit of the Union including economic and monetary union, the environment, agriculture and fisheries, social policy, competition policy, external trade, the single market, foreign and security policy, and asylum and immigration affairs unless such matters are deemed by a double qualified majority of the Council (or the Assembly) to be better dealt with at a subsidiary level of government.

Finally, the Constitution should only come into force after it has been approved by a two-thirds majority of the EP and by a simple majority of citizens in each member state of the Union.

I do not claim that the above is an adequate constitution. What it does show, however, is that basic principles can be outlined in fewer than a thousand words.

What is needed now is for a Constitutional Assembly to be appointed from the parliaments of the member states and the European Parliament to examine seriously the drafting of a European constitution which can then be put before the people of Europe in a referendum for their acceptance or rejection. If we are to move away from the original "Brilliant Conspiracy" of the founders of modern Europe and avoid a new conspiracy by those nationalists who have failed to learn the lessons of Europe's violent past, it is vital to capture the imagination and real commitment of the people of this marvellous continent.

Bibliography

General Books on the EU

Bainbridge, Timothy and Teasdale, Anthony, *The Penguin Companion to the European Union*, (London: Penguin, 1996)

Budd, Stanley A, *The EEC: A Guide to the Maze*, (London: Kogan Page, 1985)

Crisis or Opportunity – The Discussion Papers of the Jean Monnet Group of Experts, (Hull: Centre for European Studies, University of Hull). This set of papers by leading academic writers on European Affairs covers major policy issues facing the EU.

Building the Union: reform of the institutions; *Security of the Union*; *State of the Union*; *Towards the Single Currency* – all published London: Federal Trust for Education and Research, 1995/6.

Papers and reports relating to the IGC

Baird, Nick, *The Government's IGC Overview*, (London: Foreign and Commonwealth Office, 1996)

European Movement, *Reform of the European Union – Proposals of the European Movement for British Policy Towards the Intergovernmental Conference of 1996*, (London: 1994)

Fagiolo, Silvio, *The Italian Presidency of the EU and the IGC*, (London: Royal Institute for International Affairs, 1996)

Group of the European Liberal, Democratic and Reform Party, *Proposals on the 1996 IGC*, (Brussels: 1995)

Hughes, Kirsty, 'The 1996 intergovernmental conference and EU enlargement', in *International Affairs*, vol 72, no 1, January 1996

Lamers, Karl, *A German Agenda for the European Union*, (London: Federal Trust and the Konrad Adenauer Stiftung, 1994)

Lamers, Karl and Schäubler, Wolfgang, *CDU/CSU-Fraktion des Deutschen Bundestages (Reflections on European Policy)*, (Bonn: 1994)

The Reflection Group's Reports, (Messina: June 1995, and Brussels: December 1995)

Turin European Council, Presidency Conclusions (March 1996)

Florence European Council, Presidency Conclusions, (June 1996)

Enlarging the Union

Commission of the European Communities, *Reinforcing Political Union and Preparing for Enlargement*, (Brussels: 1996)

Commission of the European Communities, *Towards a Closer Association with the Countries of Central and Eastern Europe*, (Copenhagen: 1993)

Michalski, Anna and Wallace, Helen, *Europe: The Challenge of Enlargement*, (London: Royal Institute of International Affairs, 1992)

Multi-speed Europe

Janning, Josef and Weidenfeld, Werner, 'Europe's States Need a Strategy of Differentiated Integration' in *International Herald Tribune*, 21 January 1996

Maclay, Michael, *Multi-Speed Europe?*, (London: Royal Institute for International Affairs, 1992)

Vibert, Frank, *Strctured Flexibility in the European Union*, (London: European Policy Forum, August 1996)

Federalism

A European Constitutional Settlement – Draft Report by the European Constitutional Group, (London: European Policy Forum, 1993)

Hamilton, Alexander, Madison, James and Jay, John, *The Federalist Papers* (United States and Canada: A Bantam Classic, 1988). (First published 1787-88)

Handy, Charles, 'Nothing to Fear from the F-word' in *The Independent*, February 1996

Handy, Charles, *The Age of Unreason*, (London: Arrow Books, 1995)

Handy, Charles, *The Empty Raincoat*, (London: Arrow Books, 1995)

Miller, Gary, *Nationalism and Federalism in the EC Institutions and Federalist Movement*, (Paper presented at the 9th International Seminar on European Union, Federalism and Democracy, Ventotene, 1992)

Roberts, John C. de V., *World Federalism during the sixties and seventies*, (Arundel: New England College, 1989)

Wheare, K. C. 'What Federal Government Is' in Ransom, Patrick (ed.), *Studies in Federal Planning*, (London: Macmillan, 1943)

A constitution for Europe

Hermann Report on *Constitution of the European Union*, (European Parliament, Committee on Institutional Affairs)

Millar, David, *The Reform of Constitutional relations between the European Community Institutions*, (University of Edinburgh)

Pinder, John, *Federalists and the European Constitution* (report on a joint seminar of the Federal Trust and the Union of European Federalists, 1993)

Economic and Monetary Union

Centre for Economic Policy Research, *European Economic Perspectives*, (London: April 1996)

European Monetary Institute, *Report on the transition to the Euro,* (Paris: AMUE Office, 1996)

European Monetary Union for Business, *Newsletters* 1995-1996

Federal Trust Evidence to the House of Lords, *Making economic and monetary union work,* (1996)

Hirsch, Michael, 'Dreading economic and monetary union', in *Newsweek,* January 1996

The Kingsdown Enquiry, Report by the Action Centre for Europe Working Group on the Implications of Monetary Union for Britain

Sampson, Anthony 'A worthless world of money', in *The Independent,* November 1994

European Law

Collins, Lawrence, *European Law in the UK*, (London, Dublin, Edinburgh: Butterworths, 4th edition, 1990)

Hartley, T. C., *The Foundations of European Law*, (Oxford: Oxford University Press, 2nd edition, 1991)

Mathijsen, P. S. R. F., *A Guide to European Communty Law*, (London: Sweet & Maxwell, 5th edition, 1990)

History of the Union

Bond, Martyn, Smith, Julie and Wallace, William, (eds), *Eminent Europeans*, (London: Greycoat Press, 1996)

Fontaine, Pascal, *Jean Monnet, a grand design for Europe*, (Luxembourg: European Documentation, 1988)

Waterlow, Charlotte and Evans, Archibald, *Europe 1945-1970*, (Methuen Educational Ltd, 1973)

Weigall, David and Stirk, Peter, (eds), *The Origins and Development of the European Community*, (Leicester and London: Leicester University Press, 1992)

Political memoirs

Ian Gilmour, *Dancing with Dogma*, (London: Simon & Schuster Ltd, 1992)

Jenkins, Roy, *European Diary*, (London: Collins, 1989)

Governments and constitutions

Dicey, A. V., *An Introduction to the Study of the Law of the Constitution*, (Basingstoke and London: MacMillan Education, 10th edition, 1985). (First published 1885)

Hutton, Will, *The State We're In*, (London: Jonathan Cape, 1995)

Jenkins, W. Ivor, *The British Constitution*, (Cambridge: Cambridge University Press, 1962)

Marr, Andrew, *Ruling Britannia*, (London: Michael Joseph, 1995)

Mount, Ferdinand, *The British Constitution Now*, (London: Mandarin, 1993)

Osborne, David and Gaebler, Ted, *Reinventing Government*, (London: Plume, 1993)

The author has also used information contained in numerous publications published by the European Documentation Centre, Luxembourg. Parts of the chapters on the history of the European Union and the institutions are reprinted from the author's *Simple Guide to Maastricht*, published by the European Movement, 1993.

Index

D

A BRILLIANT CONSPIRACY?